C0-DKO-534

Home Security

by Charles Dunne
with Richard V. Nunn

Copyright © 1975 by Oxmoor House, Inc.
Book Division of the Progressive Farmer Company
P.O. Box 2463, Birmingham, Alabama 35202

All rights reserved. No part of this book may be
reproduced in any form or by any means without
the prior written permission of the Publisher, ex-
cepting brief quotes used in connection with re-
views written specifically for inclusion in a maga-
zine or newspaper.

Library of Congress Catalog Card Number: 75–12126

Manufactured in the United States of America

First Printing 1975

Home Security

Editor: Candace C. Franklin
Cover Photograph: Taylor Lewis
Inside Photography: Mike Hilts

Introduction

Once upon a time, you could dig a wide moat around your castle and pull up the drawbridge to make yourself safe and secure. Moats and drawbridges are a bit obsolete now and so are castles, but the need for a secure haven for rest after the day's battle is not.

Whether your particular haven is an apartment, an average house, or an extensive estate, you need to know that it is protected against burglars and safe from fire and accidents. This book guides you in detecting the vulnerable places in your home and suggests hundreds of ways, large and small, to make it safer.

Aside from giving you greater peace of mind, good home security could save you money. You may get a discount on your insurance, for example, or you may decrease the number of medical bills and trips to the hospital emergency room. And you may avoid some lost work days.

The cost of making your home safer can run anywhere from zero up to several thousand dollars, depending on what your particular situation is and what steps are necessary to get the kind of security you want. If you go as far as installing a deluxe and elaborate burglar/fire alarm system, the bill will be high. Otherwise the cost of securing your home is nominal, and expenses can be distributed among a variety of small projects.

Your home can be safer within an hour after you read this book. You will become aware of dozens of hazardous situations you have lived with—and can now correct them quickly. Many of these hazards may seem inconsequential, but all of them are really tiny disasters waiting for a time to happen.

Making sure the door between the house and the garage is locked, for example, may foil a burglar tonight. Or grounding a three-pronged plug—a job that takes less than 30 seconds and requires only a screwdriver—may prevent a serious electrical accident.

These first efforts will cost you nothing. Next, you can make a series of minor investments—a peephole for the front and back doors or good window locks. Each improvement that helps frustrate a burglar, reduce the possibility of a fire, or eliminate a potential accident raises your security level.

Later, for somewhat larger investments, you may proceed to safer door locks, new and sturdier doors, or an intercom system. Or you may wish to install fire warning devices, outdoor lights, or bathroom grab bars.

Ultimately, you may opt for a complete alarm system, installed by professionals. Many people don't need this much protection; the purpose of this book is to help you decide exactly how much security you need, and then show you how to get it.

The first step on the road to efficient home security is to *think safety*. The security of your home doesn't depend nearly as much on your monetary investment as it does on your attitude. When you think safety, you get safety, and safety is security.

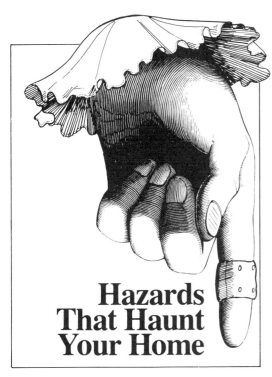

Hazards That Haunt Your Home

Your house or apartment seems serene and secure at the moment, and you'd like to keep it that way. That's why you're reading this book.

But every house, even when serene, is a haunted house—haunted by the ghosts of big and little disasters waiting to happen. One spook may be a tiny rip in the carpeting at the head of the stairs. Another may be a small pile of rags you used for refinishing a chair last week. Yet another may be an unlocked window on the second floor.

Our job in this book is to identify these hazardous spectres, make them plainly visible, and then find ways to send them out into the night. You needn't go as far as performing the rites of exorcism over a rip in the carpet, but you can at least tack it down before someone trips on it.

The major hazards which haunt every house are burglary, fire, and accidents. Your security depends on how well you have them under control. If you are like most of us, you have been ignoring the possibility of hazards occurring, or have become so accustomed to living with them that you no longer recognize the danger.

BURGLARY

Every 15 seconds a burglary occurs somewhere in the United States. In some urban areas, burglary and robbery have driven people off the streets and out of neighborhoods. Even in pleasant, low-crime suburbs and rural communities, burglaries are rising sharply. According to the FBI's Uniform Crime Report, in one year burglaries in urban centers increased 4%, while they zoomed 10% in cities with a population under 50,000 and 12% in towns of under 10,000 people. Burglaries in suburban areas jumped 10% and in rural areas 8½%.

The burglary rate varies from state to state. Nevada has had the highest rate in the nation with 2,149 burglaries per 100,000 population. North Dakota has been the lowest with 383 per 100,000 population. All told, 2,540,000 burglaries were reported in one year in the 50 states. We don't know how many have gone unreported. Here are some examples of the number of burglaries per 100,000 population in other states:

Florida	1,857	North Carolina	892
Alabama	882	Virginia	825
Georgia	1,268	New York	1,296
Illinois	1,025	California	1,979
Louisiana	962	Tennessee	1,009

No place is safe from burglary now. The police are fighting it, but they need help. Our police chief commented, "More manpower might help, but that isn't the real need. We need help from the people themselves. They tend to be relaxed about security in their homes until there is a burglary next door; then they panic. If they would think about security now, they could make it a lot tougher for burglars, and that would make our job easier."

The police chief described a recent burglary in his town. On returning home from school one day, a 12-year-old boy discovered the TV set missing. His mother had been shopping since noon but had locked the house before she left. There were no signs of forced entry, and no clue as to how the burglar got in.

The investigating officer was puzzled. He interviewed the boy, who told him, "The house was locked when I came home from school. I guess the burglars locked up when they left."

"Did you use your house key to get in?" the officer asked.

"Oh no," the boy replied. "I don't have a key. I lose them. Mother left it in the mailbox and put a note on the door so I'd know where it was."

The story is funny and dumb, but true. All too often people just don't worry about security. Windows and doors are left unlocked all the time; front doors are bolted and barred while back doors are left open; garage doors are left open while the rest of the house is locked.

Home security is up to each one of us—make it tough for a burglar to get in. "Good locks and a tight house may not stop every burglar," the chief said, "but they will stop or at least discourage a good many—and slow all of them down. That gives the police a chance to do some good."

How the Burglar Selects His Target

The professional burglar is very good at his work. He can defeat almost any lock or alarm system; when he decides to break in, he's hard to stop. But there aren't a lot of real pros, and most of them are pretty picky about the houses they enter. They don't do a job until they've cased a house thoroughly and are sure of a good haul.

The pro does a lot of research. He talks to people in bars, at gas stations, on delivery trucks, and in stores. He finds out who has bought valuable things, where they are located, and he finds out about the locks and security systems.

Don't talk about your valuables; don't brag or display them. Keep your prize-winning coin collection a private matter. Don't let the world know you are planning a trip until you get back home. Don't let strangers into your house where they can see what you have. This is the kind of information that gets to the pro and helps him to pick his next target.

The majority of burglars are not professionals. The amateur is much less selective in his work than a pro. Spotting a house that looks deserted, he'll stop and make a fast entry. He is satisfied with loot he can carry—money, a TV set, silver—and he is frustrated by sophisti-cated locks or alarms. He may defeat them, but he is slow and clumsy and needs time.

The burglar's favorite tool is the "jimmy"; he can open almost anything with it. You know it as a pinch bar or crow bar; one end is flattened and thin so it can be forced into a narrow space.

Many burglars favor using a plastic card, which they can slip between the door and the jamb and open ordinary beveled latches. This is known in the trade as "loiding," from the days when the cards were made of celluloid.

Picking locks is very big with television thieves, but not as popular with actual burglars—not because they can't do it, but because they can break in much faster with a good jimmy. You should worry less about whether or not your lock is pick-proof and more about whether or not you have a dead bolt latch, a tight door frame, and a sound, heavy door.

Besides the professionals and amateurs, there are two other classes of burglars: drug addicts and kids looking for a thrill. Drug addicts are dangerous and unpredictable. They are clumsy burglars, driven by the monkey on their backs. They are less cautious than other breeds of burglars and are apt to do anything to get money to support a habit which may cost $100 a day or more.

Kids by and large gain entry because they know the house and its inhabitants. They know when the house is vacant and where it is unlocked. These young burglars usually leave telltale signs of their ineptness. Their work is marked by the kind of items they take and by the fact that they often indulge in senseless destruction and vandalism.

Preventing Burglaries

What any burglar wants is a quick entry, peace and quiet while he works in the house, and a quick exit. If the door he tries to jimmy resists for long, he'll probably move to another door or a window. If two or three of these resist, he will find another house. Unfortunately, the majority of doors and windows don't offer much resistance.

The burglar usually prefers to work where he can't be seen, especially if he has to spend any time making his entry. A home that is well lighted at night is less attractive as a target.

Burglar alarms are effective because they make noise. If the alarm is tripped during entry, the burglar must either try to silence the noise or grab what he can and hurry away. The peace and quiet he needs to go through the house properly is disturbed.

Burglary was once considered a nighttime occupation, but in recent years this has changed. Today, more than half of the burglaries take place during the day. And nearly half of the entries are made through the front door of the house. One reason is that front doors generally are so easy to get through that a burglar can walk up to one in the daytime and be inside the house before any of the neighbors become suspicious. A quick pry with the jimmy or a fast thrust with the card, a sharp push with the shoulder, and he's in. Neither the door nor the daylight frustrates him at all. Doors can, and should, be made to deter would-be intruders.

There are a number of philosophies concerning the best way to protect a house. Some alarms are set to detect a burglar walking across a room—but in this case he is already in the house. This raises the possibility of a dangerous confrontation with the burglar that would be better avoided. The idea is to keep the burglar outside instead of confronting him after he gains entry. The best philosophy is to "protect the perimeter"; concentrate on fortifying the security at the outer edges of your house—secure doors, locks, windows, and provide outdoor lighting. Later chapters deal in detail with the security of your doors and windows and types of exterior lighting you may use.

In reviewing the security of your home, keep in mind that you should avoid burglary incidents if possible and make them difficult ventures if they should happen. Here are some good rules to follow:

1. *Don't attract burglars.* Keep your life to yourself. Don't make your valuables known to others. Don't permit your possessions to be easily seen through your windows. Don't talk about your travels or your schedule. In fact, make your schedule erratic. Don't arrive home at exactly the same hour every day. Vary your timing.

2. *Make it difficult to get into your house.* Good locks, good doors, locked windows, alarms, lights, plus the habit of always locking up, even when you go next door for coffee, will make your home tough for a burglar. If the house is being cased, the alert burglar will note your conscientious habits and good locks. Unless he figures you have something really worth his making an extra effort, he might well transfer his affections to someone else's castle.

3. *Be alert and suspicious.* Watch for strange cars parked in the vicinity of your home; the driver may be casing his next job. If you get a lot of strange telephone calls, too many wrong number calls, for example, be suspicious. A burglar may be trying to find out when your house is unoccupied. Be leery of salesmen or others who find it necessary to see the inside of your house.

4. *Make your house look occupied at all times.* When you aren't home, use timers to switch lights on and off and to turn radios on. Don't let mail or newspapers accumulate. Keep garage doors closed when the cars aren't in the garage. These rules are important when you are traveling, but they can be equally important when you are away from the house for only a couple of hours.

Guns

Some people feel that they must keep a handgun in their homes to protect themselves against intruders. Authorities on home security generally disagree with this idea for several reasons.

To be useful in a burglary situation, a gun must be kept loaded and readily accessible. Usually, homeowners keep the gun in a nightstand beside the bed. Unfortunately, guns kept in this manner are also accessible to children. The large number of firearm accidents involving children attest to the dangers of keeping a loaded gun on hand.

A gun doesn't become useful until you actually confront an intruder with it. If the intruder is armed, such a confrontation can easily turn into a shooting situation in which you run a high risk of injury or death. Many people who keep guns for protection don't maintain their proficiency in the use of weapons. Too often they are nervous when handling a gun; this nervousness would prove to be a severe disadvantage in a confrontation.

By weighing the advantages against the disadvantages, security experts believe that in most cases a gun would bring more danger than security to homeowners who keep them for security reasons. A good perimeter alarm system that is designed to frustrate the burglar's entry or drive him away from the house would provide the homeowner with better, and safer, security.

Watchdogs

If a dog is any kind of watchdog at all, he acts as an excellent alarm system with a built-in set of very perceptive sensors. Dogs will almost always bark and sound an alarm when strangers approach, when they hear noises they don't understand, or when they feel heat or smell smoke. Even a small family pet can be a very useful part of any home's security.

A larger dog, particularly one of a breed noted for aggressiveness, such as a German shepherd or a Doberman pinscher, is an even greater security asset. A burglar would not only be annoyed at the dog's barking, but he would be in fear of being attacked by the dog once he has gained entry into the home. When sizing up a neighborhood, most burglars would pass up homes guarded by dogs of this type.

Even if a dog were kept in a run somewhere on the property, but not in the house, his furious barking at the approach of a burglar would warn the homeowner—and probably the whole neighborhood—that something was wrong.

But then there are the friendly dogs who love everyone but the mailman. If you have a big, happy, friendly pooch who would probably welcome Jack the Ripper at 2 o'clock in the morning, you might consider installing a burglar alarm system. The fact is that not all dogs are watchdogs. Some are just marvelous companions.

You can, of course, buy a trained watchdog. Many of these dogs are vicious attackers and are great in some security situations. But by and large, such dogs should not live in a family environment. They can be dangerous.

FIRE

Fire is no less a hazard to your home security than burglary. In the United

---

Causes of Fire in the Home

Cooking and heating appliances, including grease fires, furnace-caused fires	24.1%
Careless smoking	17.7%
Electricity and appliances, including faulty appliances and overheating of wire due to draw of excessive current through circuit	13.8%
Children with matches	9.7%
Flammable liquids, usually from faulty storage	9.2%
Faulty chimneys, cracked, unclean chimneys, and unguarded fireplaces	4.6%
Clothing ignited, most often involving children— birthday candles a frequent cause	4.2%
All other causes	16.7%

Smoking and improper use of electrical appliances account for ⅓ of all home fires. These are the result of carelessness and can be avoided.

States, 1,500 homes burn each day, destroying property and causing many families to suffer financial problems, injuries, disability, and death. Most fires can be prevented.

Careless smoking habits cause over 17% of all home fires. For the most part, this carelessness means smoking in bed, on a sofa, or in an upholstered chair. Such fires cause a high number of fatalities because the smoker is often dozing right where the fire starts and dies of smoke inhalation without ever awakening. Firemen, who see its tragic results so often, consider smoking in bed the deadliest habit you can have.

Nearly a quarter of all home fires are started by furnaces, heating appliances, and stoves. Grease fires in the kitchen are a major contributor to the number of fires in this category. Fires caused by children playing with matches and cigarette lighters cause 9.7% of all home fires. Together, the three causes of fire mentioned here account for half of the home fires in the country.

ACCIDENTS

Over 60,000 persons die each year in accidents not involving automobiles. Of these deaths, 26,000 are the results of accidents in the home. The National Safety Council reports that 4 million persons are disabled for a day or more annually by home accidents.

The largest category of home accidents is falls. Two-thirds of the fatal falls in the home take place at floor level; the victims trip over a throw rug, an end table, or a toy on the floor. Stairways, surprisingly enough, are in second place. Wet bathroom and kitchen floors are high on the dangerous fall list, as are slippery bath tubs.

Older persons are often victims of falling because of failing eyesight and deteriorating muscular strength and coordination. If you or someone in your home is over 65, pay special attention to hazards in the house which can cause falls.

Statistics tell a different kind of story about accidents in the home involving children. The leading cause of accidental death is fire and burns, but the two leading causes of child injuries are home playground equipment and cleaning agents. Young children need to be supervised when they are out on the home gym. And you should put a lock on the cabinet where you keep detergents, ammonia, window cleaner, and other cleaning agents. Just closing the cabinet door on them isn't enough. For a long time safety experts have been advising the need for locks on medicine cabinets. It now appears that the cleaning agent storage shelf may be an even greater hazard.

Home Accident Deaths

	1950	1960	1970
Total accidental deaths	29,000	28,000	27,000
Falls	14,800	12,300	9,700
Fires, burns	5,000	6,350	5,600
Suffocations, ingestion of foreign objects	not available	1,700	1,800
Poison by liquids, solids	1,300	1,350	3,000
Firearms	950	1,200	1,100

National Safety Council

These figures indicate that total accidental deaths in the home have decreased slightly over a 30-year span. That's the good news. The bad news is that deaths by poisoning and firearm accidents have almost doubled.

Deaths by Accident

	All Ages	Under 5 years	5–14 years
Total, all types of accidents	114,638	6,594	8,203
Motor vehicle accidents	54,633	1,915	4,159
Falls	16,926	340	196
Drowning	7,860	890	1,550
Fires, burns	6,718	848	609
Ingestion of food, objects	2,753	906	122
Firearms	2,406	93	413
Poison by liquids, solids	3,679	226	44
Poison by gas	1,620	34	58

National Safety Council

These figures tell some tragic stories. Over 60,000, including 8,700 children, persons died in one year in accidents other than those involving motor vehicles. Falls account for the majority of home accidents. Note that 500 children died in firearms accidents, the best proof that guns should be kept under lock and key.

Principal Types of Fatal Accidents to the Elderly in One Year

Falls, often due to failing eyesight and poor muscular strength and coordination	12,000
Motor vehicles	7,400
Fires, burns, and deaths associated with fire Older persons often have difficulty in escaping from a burning area	2,000
Inhalation and ingestion of food or other objects, causing suffocation	700
Poisoning by solids, liquids, gases—often carbon monoxide poisoning from faulty heating units	650
Drowning	500
Disabling injuries of at least one day's duration resulting from all types of accidents	800,000

National Safety Council

These statistics cover persons age 65 and over; 4% of these accidents occur in private homes, 26% involve motor vehicles, 26% occur in public places, and 4% take place at work.

Home Accidents Involving Children 0–14 Years in One Year	
Home playground equipment injuries	Over 100,000
Cleaning agent injuries	22,200
Deaths from fire, burns	1,300
Deaths from suffocation, including smothering by bed clothes, thin plastics, cave-ins, confinement in closed places	640
Deaths from suffocation due to ingested objects	550
Deaths from firearms	400
Deaths from accidental falls	350
Poisoning by solids and liquids, including household products, medicines, polishes	270
Deaths from other home accidents, including drowning, electric current, falling objects	1,170

National Safety Council

Of the 4,680 deaths shown, 3,330 were children under the age of 5.

Home security begins at the front door. The first rule is: don't open the door unless you know who's on the other side.

This lovely home in an urban area was made secure by the use of ornate iron grilles on the first floor windows and high iron fencing with a locked gate at the back of the house.

Apartment security has special problems. It requires not only an effort on your part but also cooperation among tenants and between tenants and landlord.

Left:
Burglars look for windows and doors which are screened from the view of passers-by and neighbors by a heavy growth of bushes and trees. Open landscaping makes for better security.

Right:
Basement windows are often neglected in home security, particularly if they are small or open into a window well. But even small windows will admit a burglar. The ironwork on this window helps secure the home from intruders and is an attractive architectural touch.

Back doors usually can't be seen from the street and are a favorite target for burglars, particularly at night. This door is an open invitation to burglary; it has a single key-in-knob type lock and windows near the lock. Entry is simple; the burglar has only to break the glass pane, reach in, and unlock the door. He can be in the house in less than 15 seconds. Back doors should be well lighted and have a secure door and lock arrangement.

Hazards That Haunt Your Home   13

Improving Security

SECURITY STEPS TO TAKE RIGHT NOW

Too many of us think that security consists of elaborate burglar alarm systems or armed guards on round-the-clock duty. Actually, at home, security is destroyed by a collection of relatively small hazards. To improve security, first identify each hazard, then eliminate it.

The projects suggested in this chapter can be carried out in a few hours. At first glance, you may think them simple and too obvious. That is the problem with them; they are so simple and obvious that we tend to overlook them every day.

Each hazard described below is responsible for a higher-than-average number of security mishaps; some of them rate among the highest on lists of hazards maintained by such organizations as the National Safety Council.

Look at each photograph and ask yourself, "Is this a problem in my home?" If the answer is "yes," do something about it now.

Lock all of your doors every time you leave the house, even if you are only running next door for a few minutes. Entry through unlocked doors accounts for 6% of all burglaries and gives thrill-seeking kids and vandals the opportunity they are looking for.

You are looking through the front window of a home at an expensive radio. Place all such valuable and particularly tempting items where they cannot be seen from the outside.

This empty garage fairly screams, "We're not at home!" A burglar cruising through the neighborhood looking for employment will get the message. Keep garage doors closed when you are at home and when you're away; don't make things easy for criminals.

A police bar is an excellent way to protect a door. It makes forcible entry difficult and is especially useful in an apartment because it doesn't have to be attached to anything. Because of the angle at which it rests against the door, it is actually better than a heavy piece of furniture shoved against the door.

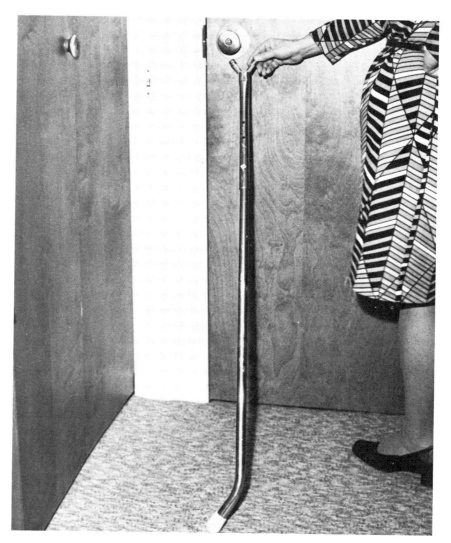

Use a small motorized etching tool to put your name or other identification on all items—radios, cameras, TV sets—which can be easily carried away. Display near exterior doors the warning label which comes with some of the tools or can be obtained from many police departments. The police are enthusiastic about Operation Identification; it enables them to identify and return stolen articles when they apprehend a suspicious character. The burglar can't claim he just borrowed the radio from his Aunt Minnie. Burglars tend to avoid homes utilizing Operation Identification.

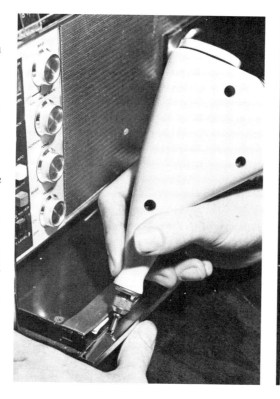

We have joined
OPERATION
IDENTIFICATION

WARNING

ALL ITEMS OF VALUE ON THESE PREMISES HAVE BEEN MARKED FOR READY IDENTIFICATION BY LAW ENFORCEMENT AGENCIES.

11213   MOISTEN THIS SIDE

Sliding glass doors are a major source of home accidents; a person can walk through the glass, thinking the door is open when it is not. Eliminate this hazard by making the glass visible. A quick method is to use plastic tape on the door, as shown here. A prettier alternative is to buy decals and apply them to the glass.

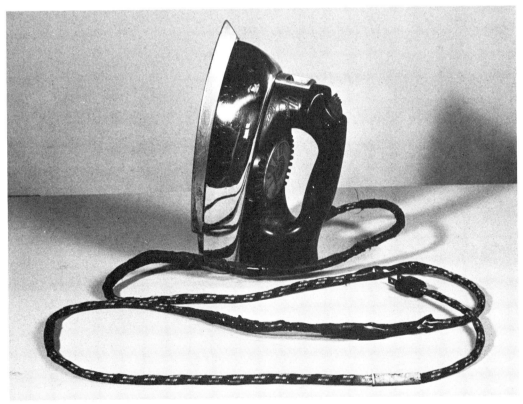

Don't use electrical appliances that are damaged in any way. This applies especially to heating appliances. The cord on this iron has frayed and has been repeatedly patched with tape, representing a potential fire hazard or serious electric shock. The iron should not be used again until the cord has been replaced. Electric iron replacement cords can be purchased at any hardware store.

Ashtrays look innocent enough, but the poorly-designed ones are a serious fire hazard. A safe ashtray, such as the one on the left, has prongs, fingers, or some other effective method of gripping the cigarette in such a manner that it will burn out without falling to the table top or to the carpeting. The ashtray on the right is dangerous. A cigarette on its lip will fall from the tray after burning for a few minutes.

Never, under any circumstances, should you carry gasoline in a can in your car. This rule applies to the heavy-duty, safe-looking cans as well as to the flimsy ones. Firemen have been saying for years that this was a lethal practice. During a gasoline shortage the number of auto fires and explosions skyrocket because people insist on carrying reserve fuel in cans in their trunk. If you are transporting gasoline in a can, a collision can turn your car into a fire bomb. Gasoline fumes can collect in the car and be ignited by the lighting of a cigarette or by a spark from an electric switch. Carrying gasoline in a car isn't an ordinary hazard; it is extremely dangerous.

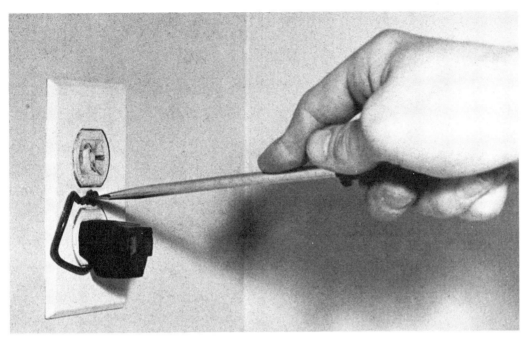

Do you find those three-prong plugs a nuisance? You never have one when you need it, and when you find one, you haven't time to connect the ground wire to the screw in the center of the wall outlet plate. Take the time. This connection grounds any tool or appliance and protects you against a fatal electric shock if the appliance casing becomes alive with electricity. In such cases, the current passes through the ground wire and not through you. Fatal shocks of this type account for more than 1,000 deaths annually. Always attach the little wire or metal ear to the center screw in the wall plate. It takes only a minute to do it with a screwdriver. Better yet, replace other types of wall outlets with three-hole outlets. There is no need to shut off your electricity to do the job; just be sure your hands are dry.

The door between the garage and the house may be the most neglected door in your home. Conscientious homeowners carefully double lock the front and back doors and toddle off to bed, frequently forgetting the door to the garage. Put the same locks on this door that you put on other exterior doors. Entry into a garage is often easy for a burglar, and once inside he can work on the door to the house without fear of being spotted. If you forgot to lock the door, his work becomes incredibly easy.

Falls of any type top the list of home accidents and account for the greatest number of fatalities. Objects left on stairways or near the tops of stairs are guaranteed to contribute to these statistics. Litter on stairs is difficult to see when you are coming down, especially if you wear glasses or are carrying an armload of something. Basement stairways are especially evil places, since they often collect laundry on its way to the washing machine. Keep stairways clear at all times.

The outdoor charcoal grill, portable variety, rates high on the list of accident causers. Three kinds of accidents head the list, not including indigestion from badly cooked meals. The first is the tipped over grill which can do terrible damage to your legs. Make sure your grill is stable and sits firmly on level ground, preferably on cement. The second type of accident involving grills is the squirt of lighter fluid applied to hot coals. The flash of fire that results can char your hands and ignite your clothes. Finally, there are the fumes that collect when you attempt to use a charcoal grill indoors. Some people have tried this when a storm has knocked out their electricity, and they have died from the deadly fumes. When charcoal is used indoors, as it is in some steak houses, a ventilator is located directly over the grill and operates as long as the coals are burning. Keep your grill out in the yard.

SECURITY QUOTIENT CHECK LIST

Hazards haunt every home, but you can get rid of most of them and not have to spend much money to do it. The following is a Security Quotient Check List, a form to help you evaluate the security needs in your home. Review the form now, but wait until you've read more of the book before making any evaluations.

Sealing the Perimeter

yes no

- ☐ ☐ Deadbolt locks are on every exterior door
- ☐ ☐ Locks are modern, working, and reliable
- ☐ ☐ Door chain guards are on every exterior door
- ☐ ☐ Doors fit tightly in their frames to protect against jimmying
- ☐ ☐ Doors are tight against stop molding
- ☐ ☐ Window panes in and near entry doors are sheet plastic, not glass
- ☐ ☐ Doors with window panes have locks on both the inside and outside of the door; key is needed to open door from either side
- ☐ ☐ Entryways are well lighted at night
- ☐ ☐ Floodlights are used to illuminate the yard at night
- ☐ ☐ Windowless doors have peepholes or an intercom setup for easy identification of callers
- ☐ ☐ All shrubbery around windows and exterior doors is well trimmed
- ☐ ☐ All first floor windows have good locks that are not easily defeated
- ☐ ☐ Second floor windows with access from the roof or porch have secure locks
- ☐ ☐ You know where every key to every lock is
- ☐ ☐ Your key chain does not have an ID tag stating your name, address, and phone number
- ☐ ☐ Exterior doors are solid wood and sturdy (hollow and weak paneled doors should be replaced)
- ☐ ☐ All sliding doors have a bar lock or a length of broomstick to secure them
- ☐ ☐ The garage door has a secure lock, and you use it
- ☐ ☐ Infrequently used entrances to your home are checked regularly
- ☐ ☐ You deal with any strangers only at the front door

Preventing Accidents

yes no

- ☐ ☐ Throw rugs have rubber undersides or non-skid strips
- ☐ ☐ Be sure stairways are clear of all objects
- ☐ ☐ All stairways have handrails
- ☐ ☐ Stairways are well lighted
- ☐ ☐ Stepladders are sturdy and in good shape
- ☐ ☐ Carpet seams are tacked down firmly, especially on stairway landings
- ☐ ☐ Plastic grip mats are on kitchen and bathroom floors or on any wet or waxed surface
- ☐ ☐ Medicine cabinets are locked and old prescriptions discarded
- ☐ ☐ Household chemicals and insecticides are stored out of sight on a high shelf or locked in a cabinet
- ☐ ☐ Aged chemicals are discarded and everything kept is well labeled
- ☐ ☐ Firearms are unloaded, locked securely in a rack, and kept separate from ammunition
- ☐ ☐ Large kitchen knives are locked in a case, not in a drawer accessible to small children
- ☐ ☐ Everyone in your family has been instructed never to squirt fire starter on a charcoal fire once it has been started
- ☐ ☐ Charcoal grills are kept outside and never used indoors where fumes are dangerous
- ☐ ☐ Bathtub and shower stalls have grab bars and non-slip mats
- ☐ ☐ Night-lights are used in bedrooms and hallways
- ☐ ☐ Furniture indoors and out has been tested for wobbles and potential upsets
- ☐ ☐ Large windows and glass patio doors are clearly marked with decals to prevent accidents

Ensuring Electrical Safety

yes no
- [ ] [ ] All lamps, lighting fixtures, and switches are in excellent condition
- [ ] [ ] Appliances with frayed, cracked, or split cords are kept out of use until they are repaired or replaced
- [ ] [ ] Each circuit contains the correct fuse size
- [ ] [ ] All appliances are at a safe distance from water; you and your family are aware that water and electricity are a deadly combination
- [ ] [ ] Your family is aware that there is a danger of electrocution when entering a flooded basement
- [ ] [ ] You know not to submerge the electrical portion of any appliance in water
- [ ] [ ] You disconnect any appliance before you attempt to repair it
- [ ] [ ] You know not to put anything behind a fuse to keep it from blowing: the fuse is your only protection and control over an enormous energy source

Fighting Fire

yes no
- [ ] [ ] You have discarded the junk accumulated in closets, basement, garage, and attic
- [ ] [ ] Things to be saved are stored or packed in boxes; combustibles are stored in metal containers
- [ ] [ ] Paint rags and old paint cans are discarded or stored in airtight containers
- [ ] [ ] A screen covers the fireplace opening
- [ ] [ ] Furniture and combustibles are at a safe distance from fireplace
- [ ] [ ] Paper towels, flammables, curtains are kept away from stove
- [ ] [ ] Stove hood is cleaned often to prevent grease buildup
- [ ] [ ] Gasoline is stored in metal container in garage, not carried in the car or stored in the house
- [ ] [ ] Radio and TV are away from the wall by several inches. TV antennas are grounded
- [ ] [ ] Extension cords are used sparingly and are run under carpets or hung by nails
- [ ] [ ] Trash is put in receptacles away from any heat source and emptied often
- [ ] [ ] All wall outlets are in excellent condition and are never overloaded
- [ ] [ ] Furnace is cleaned and checked regularly
- [ ] [ ] Ash trays are large, deep, and hold cigarettes firmly
- [ ] [ ] Your entire family has been drilled in escape routes in the event of a fire
- [ ] [ ] In a two-story home, family members have an alternate route in the event of a fire-blocked stairwell

Security at Your Doors

There is a knock on your door. You open it and a moment later find yourself forced back into the house, with one or more intruders invading your home. This kind of forcible entry will defeat any alarm system and the best of locks. The only way to protect against it is to follow sensible rules when answering the door.

Always have the safety chain in place when opening the door. If you have a peephole and an intercom system, use them before opening the door. Don't open the door unless you know who is on the other side.

Ask for official identification from delivery or service men, and examine it with the safety chain in place. Release the chain only after you are satisfied with the caller's identification. If you have an alarm system with a panic button near the door, keep your hand close to the button even after you open the door for strangers.

If you have the slightest doubt about the caller's intentions, don't open the door. Whatever the person on the other side has to offer, it can't be more important than your security. Tell him to come back at a later, specified time when you know others will be with you. If his business with you is important, he'll return at that time.

A burglar always has a good reason why you should open the door and let him in. Forget your good manners and sense of hospitality with strangers. Keep questioning and testing their identification and purpose until you are satisfied.

These rules apply to all exterior doors, not just the front door. Have the same good locks and security chains on all exterior doors. Don't neglect back doors, doors to the garage, basement doors, or the sliding glass doors to a patio.

HOW TO MAKE A DOOR BURGLAR-RESISTANT

More than half of all burglaries occur during daylight. The burglar walks calmly to your front door, trying not to attract attention; a quick glance at the lock tells him how to proceed. He will knock and then wait to see if anyone is home.

If the occupants are gone, the burglar will then surreptitiously apply a jimmy to the door to force the lock, or he will insert a plastic card between the door and the jamb to open the latch. He'll do this carefully, so that a passer-by will think he is only ringing the bell or knocking.

The jimmy is the most widely used burglary tool because it is quick and usually successful. The plastic card trick works best in hotels and apartments. Lock picking is relatively rare in home entries.

If your door has glass in it, especially small panes that are easily broken, the burglar will smash one and reach inside to open the door. At night, when he can't be seen by neighbors, he is more likely to try entry through a back door or a window, but his technique will be the same.

The burglar's technique tells you what you must do to defeat him. The door and the lock must be jimmy-proof. Any door glass should be replaced by plastic panes that are difficult to break. Even with plastic panes, doors with windows should have locks which require a key both inside and out so that even if the window is broken, the burglar can't open the door from the inside.

To be effective, a jimmy must be inserted between the door edge and the jamb. If the burglar can get leverage there, he can force the door and the jamb apart, pulling the bolt out of the strike plate. The door then swings open.

On most exterior doors, the stop and the jamb are one piece so the stop can't be pried off. The stop covers the space between the door and the jamb where the jimmy must be inserted. If the door fits tightly against the stop, it is much more difficult to get the jimmy in. If there is space between the door and the stop, the jimmy will enter easily.

To adjust the door so that it closes tightly against the stop, you will probably have to relocate the strike plate. This isn't difficult. Remove the screws holding the plate in the jamb and determine by trial and error just how far toward the stop it must be moved. After moving the plate, redrive the screws.

You may have to chisel out a little of the jamb wood behind the plate so the latch and bolt can enter easily. To make the plate secure, you may have to fill the old screw holes with wood chips dipped in glue and drive the screws into new holes after the glue has dried.

TYPES OF DOORS

There are three types of doors: solid wood, paneled, and hollow-core. A solid door is exactly that—thick, solid wood. A paneled door is made of solid wood framing (the frame is called the stile) with thinner panels inset for decorative purposes. The hollow-core door is a wood frame covered front and back with a thin skin of plywood.

The most secure door is the solid wood type. A paneled door is safe if the panels are fairly heavy and set securely in place. The hollow-core door should never be used as an exterior door. It will shatter under the impact of a good kick or a blow with the fist. Hollow-core doors offer privacy but not security.

You will sometimes find hollow-core doors used as entry doors in apartments. If this is the case in your apartment, talk to the landlord about installing a new and better door.

You can test your exterior doors by giving them a good hard kick. If a panel breaks during the test, be happy that you have discovered the weakness before a thief did. Replace the door with a sturdier one.

All glass in doors should be replaced with plastic panes for security reasons. Some states require storm doors to be glazed with plastic because of the number of serious accidents involving glass doors. A good storm door, plastic glazed, is a burglar deterrent because it is one more obstacle the intruder must get past. But don't depend on a storm door for security; it is easily forced open. Locking the storm door but leaving the main door unlocked is asking for trouble.

TYPES OF LOCKS

Locks may be divided into two basic groups: surface locks and those which are installed within or through the door. Surface locks include safety chains, sliding bolts, bars of various sorts—any lock which is fixed to the surface of the door.

The main failing of a surface lock is that it can be ripped off the door if enough force is applied. To prevent this, fasten surface locks in place with long, heavy screws coated with glue before being driven into the wood.

Every door should have a well-mounted, heavy security chain.

There are four main types of modern installed locks:

Rim locks are surface-mounted on the inside of the door; a cylinder extends through the door to the outside where the lock is opened by a key. According to most locksmiths, the most secure lock is a vertical bolt (rim type), mounted on a solid door, and equipped with an anti-pick cylinder.

Key-in-knob locks are the most common lock used by builders today. These locks are cylinder locks with the keyhole in the knob. They have a spring latch that is beveled on one side to allow the door to close. Locksmiths don't like key-in-knob locks because the knob can be forced and broken, exposing the locking mechanism. If you now have a key-in-knob lock, it would be wise to install a separate deadbolt assembly above it in the door.

Mortise locks are set in a mortise, the rectangular cavity cut into the door from the edge. They have both a spring latch and a dead bolt; the spring latch can be locked by buttons in the door edge. Most mortise locks are operated by a key from the outside and a turning knob on the inside, although you can buy models with keys on both the inside and outside for

Rim Lock

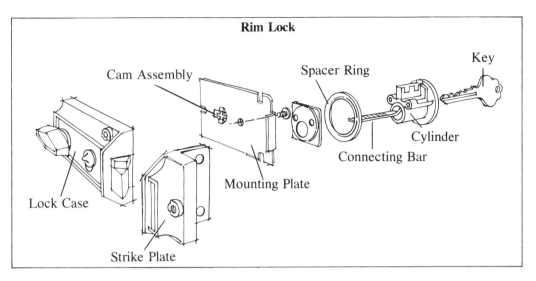

Cam Assembly — Spacer Ring — Key — Cylinder — Connecting Bar — Mounting Plate — Lock Case — Strike Plate

Key-in-Knob Lock

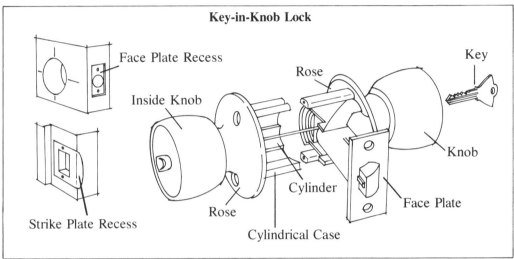

Face Plate Recess — Rose — Key — Inside Knob — Knob — Cylinder — Rose — Face Plate — Strike Plate Recess — Cylindrical Case

use in doors with windows. If you use a lock of this type, remember that you are locked in and must have a key to get out; in case of an emergency, this could be a problem. You must have a key hanging near the door but out of sight.

Deadbolt locks are bolts with squared ends, as opposed to spring latches which have beveled bolts. The beveled bolt can be opened with a plastic card pushed between the door and the jamb ("carded" or "loided"), but a deadbolt cannot be carded. If you now have key-in-knob locks, a deadbolt is a good idea as a second lock on each exterior door.

If you ask a locksmith about the safest lock to install, he'll probably tell you that a good mortised lockset is best. For top security, he might recommend the addi-

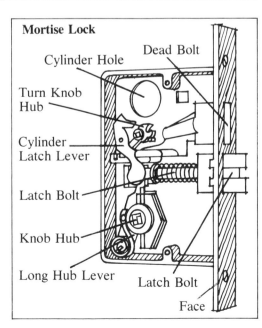

Mortise Lock

Cylinder Hole — Dead Bolt — Turn Knob Hub — Cylinder Latch Lever — Latch Bolt — Knob Hub — Long Hub Lever — Latch Bolt — Face

tion of a vertical bolt to the door as well. You'll need two keys to open the door, which is a nuisance, but you'll have a jimmy-proof, secure door.

Locks come in a variety of qualities. Examine locks on display; the machining will tell you a lot. Good locks are smooth, well-machined, and work easily. The bolt clicks home with a solid sound and will offer such features as "case-hardened steel" and "one-piece construction."

Look for a lock which has a 1-inch throw of the bolt. This length bolt will project farther into the strike plate and be much harder to jimmy than a shorter bolt. Some locks throw as little as ½ inch.

When buying a lock for an exterior door, don't be too economy minded. Spend what it takes to get the best; it may save you a bundle later. Don't buy ornamentation. Fancy finishes cost money and an expensive lock may be costly because of the finish rather than a good locking mechanism. The highest priced locks have both ornamental finishes (scrollwork, etc.) and good locking mechanisms.

Locksmiths say that worn locks are easy to defeat. If your present locks are loose and worn, consider replacing them with newer, better locks.

SECURITY AND YOUR KEYS

Do you know where every key for your house is right now? Have any been lost? Don't take chances if you can't account for some keys. Have the cylinder on the door changed, or change it yourself. A locksmith can change the keying of your present cylinders.

Don't keep house keys on the same ring with your car keys. When you park your car in a public garage and leave the keys, there is plenty of time for someone to copy them, and you'd never know about it.

When you hide a key outside of the house for someone—a poor habit—put the key in an unlikely place. The three most obvious hiding places are in the mailbox, under the door mat, and on the molding over the door. Avoid these places and put the key in a different hiding place every time; if your house is being watched, you don't want the burglar to know where to get a free and easy trip to your valuables.

Putting your name and address on a key ring may help to get it back if you lose them, but it may also direct the burglar to your house. Even after lost keys are returned, it is a good idea to change your locks.

Don't open the door until you know who's on the other side; a peephole gives you the opportunity to look first. It is most effective when coupled with an intercom system which enables you to talk to the caller as well as see him.

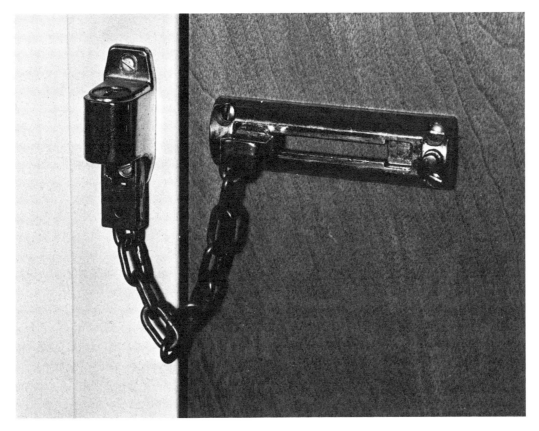

Leave the door chain on when you open the door. This chain locks with a key. When locked, the chain is shortened so that a burglar can't work his arm in through the partially open door to take the chain off.

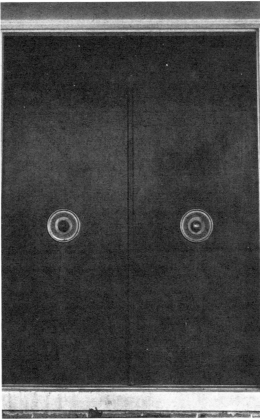

Left:
This paneled front door is only moderately secure. The panels are large and may break when kicked or hit. A door with smaller panels and more stiles would be better.

Right:
Double doors present a special security problem; there is no stop to protect the point where the doors meet. A simple wooden strip covers it here, but this could be easily pried off thus allowing a jimmy to be forced between the doors. To be safe, this door should have sliding bolts at the top and bottom of each door on the inside.

After smashing the window, a burglar can reach inside to unlock and open the door. In this case, his efforts are in vain because the door is secured by a deadbolt that is operated by a key on both the inside and the outside.

Left:
Sliding bolts on each of these double doors latch into a metal threshold. A similar pair is used at the top of the door and when all four are locked, these doors would be very difficult to force open.

Right:
The vertical bolt is considered the most effective of all locks, since it is virtually jimmy-proof. The latch housing should be screwed not only to the wall but also to the face of the door jamb.

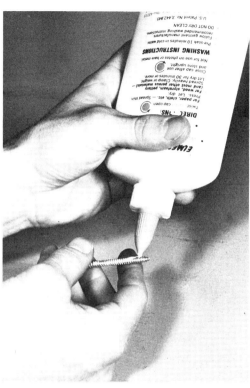

Left:
This key-in-knob lock was augmented by a deadbolt above it. You can see where an attempt was made to insert a jimmy near the deadbolt. The attempt was unsuccessful and the burglar left without entering the house.

Right:
When mounting surface locks, use long screws and coat the screw with glue before driving it in. The disadvantage of surface locks is that they can be torn from their moorings if the door is hit hard enough.

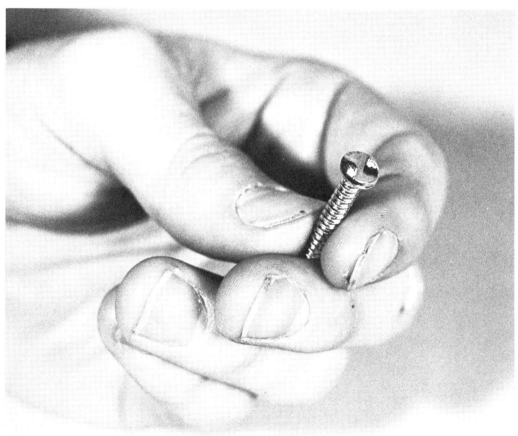

There have been cases where burglars have reached in through windows and removed the screws holding locks in place. This screw can be turned only one way; once it has been driven in, it cannot be taken out.

INSTALLING A PEEPHOLE

Left:
When installing a peephole, clamp pieces of wood to the front and the back of the door before drilling the hole. This will prevent the door wood from splintering as the drill passes through.

Right:
After the hole has been drilled, insert the two threaded parts of the peephole, one from the inside, the other from the outside. Turn them until they are tight to complete the installation.

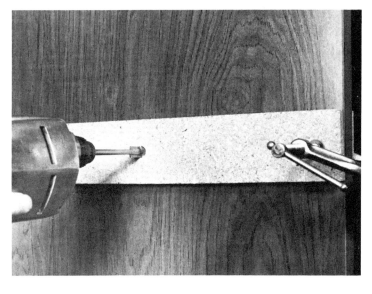
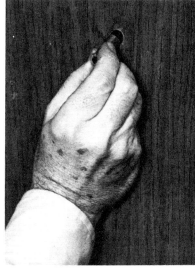

REPLACING A MORTISE LOCK

Old, worn locks are easy for burglars to defeat and should be replaced. Begin by removing the outside handle. This lock can be unscrewed from the outside, which is not a very good idea since a burglar could also dismantle it.

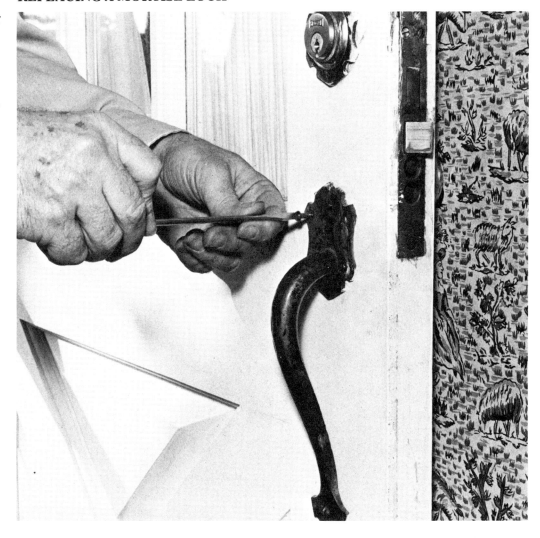

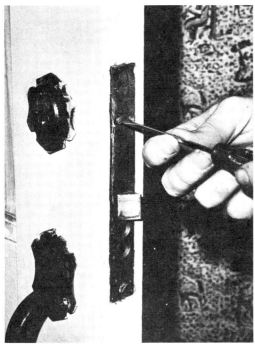
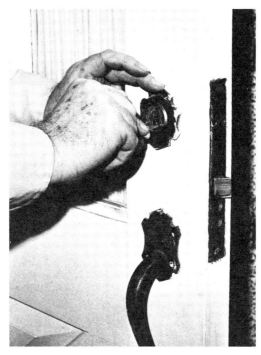

Left:
To remove the outside cylinder, first loosen the setscrew in the faceplate of the mortise housing.

Right:
Insert the key halfway into the lock. Using the key as a lever, gently unscrew the cylinder. Don't use force on the key or it may break.

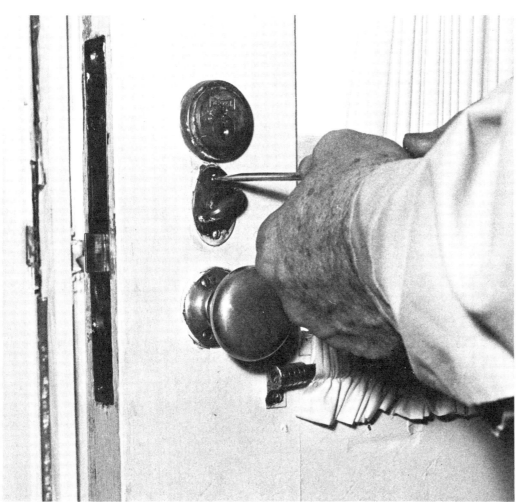

This lockset on the inside of the door has a thumb turn and an inside cylinder, but the cylinder is useless because when the lock is locked with a key, it can still be unlocked by simply turning the thumb turn. A burglar can break the window and reach in to do this. To correct the situation, replace the old lockset with a new one having cylinders inside and outside, but no thumb turn. You will have to use a key both inside and outside to unlock it. For emergencies, keep a key hanging out of sight near the door.

Remove the thumb turn plate by taking out the screws which hold it to the door, and lift out the thumb turn mechanism. Then remove the inside cylinder just as you did the outside one, using the key to turn the cylinder out of its hole.

Left:
To remove the doorknob, loosen the setscrew on the shank and thread the knob off of its spindle.

Right:
Remove the doorknob plate by removing the screws which hold it to the door.

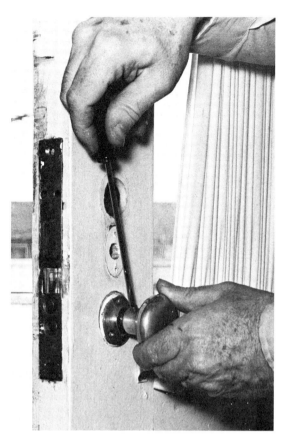
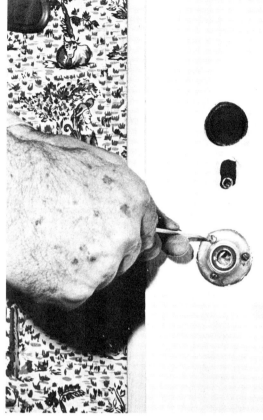

Remove the mortise lock housing by removing the screws at the top and bottom of the faceplate.

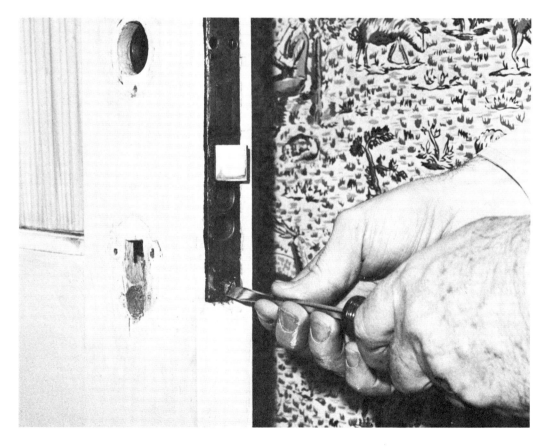

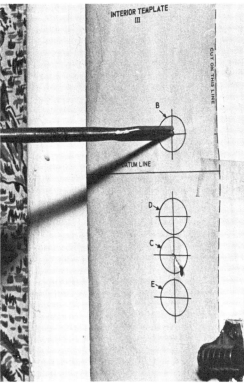

Left:
If the housing fits snugly into the mortise, use a screwdriver to pry it part way out; then pull it the rest of the way.

Right:
Begin installation of the new lock by taping the template which comes with the lock to the door. Instructions with the template tell you how to locate the datum, or reference, line to position the template properly. The new lock may have dimensions different from the old one, even though it is of the same type, so you may have to redrill the holes in the door. In extreme cases, it may be necessary to fill the old holes with plugs of wood coated with glue before redrilling.

In this case, the cylinder and doorknob holes already in the door will fit the new lock, but the mortise itself is too small. It must be chiseled out ⅛ inch wider.

Covering Holes

When installing a new lock, you must sometimes drill new holes and abandon old ones; other times, you must shift a hole only part way. The problem each time is how to cover the old or partly exposed holes. Locksmiths often cover them with something called a "patch plate" (left) or a full decorative plate (center). A variety of cylinder spacers (right) are also available to simplify the installation of the new lock. Check with your locksmith or hardware dealer.

If the new mortise housing is slightly deeper than the old, deepen the mortise with the chisel.

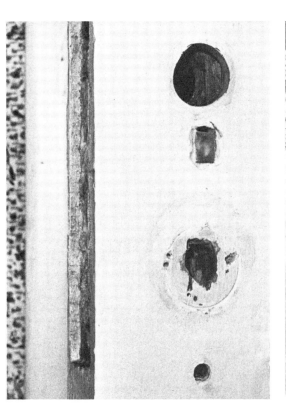
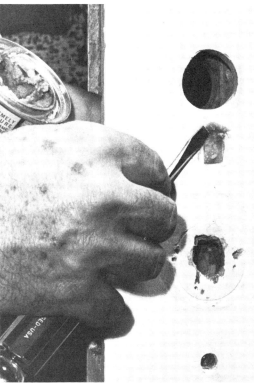

Left:
If the thumb turn hole isn't needed with the new lock, fill the hole with a small square of wood coated with glue.

Right:
Work wood filler into the hole around the wood plug with a screwdriver to complete the fill. After the filler has dried, sand it smooth, and paint it.

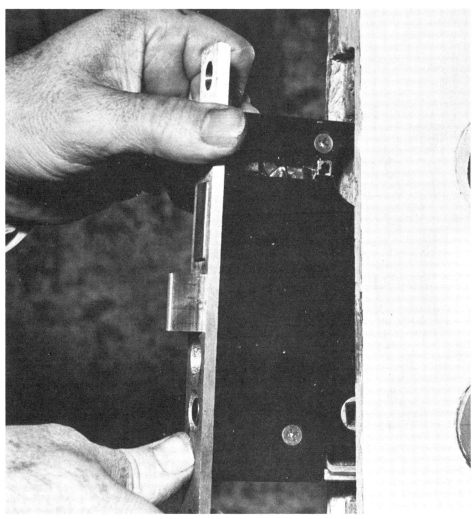

Slip the new mortise case into the widened and deepened mortise and tighten the screws which hold it in position.

Left:
Next, install the new outside handle by first drilling the required holes through the door. Every lock is different, so check the instructions for this part of the installation. If a template is provided, use it to locate the places to drill.

Right:
Position the new handle on the door. This one has guides which are inserted in the holes.

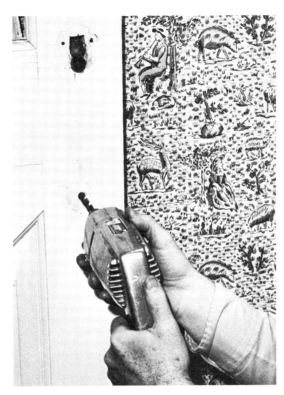
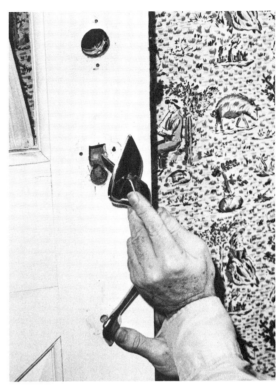

Two screws, inserted through the door from the inside, hold this outside handle in place.

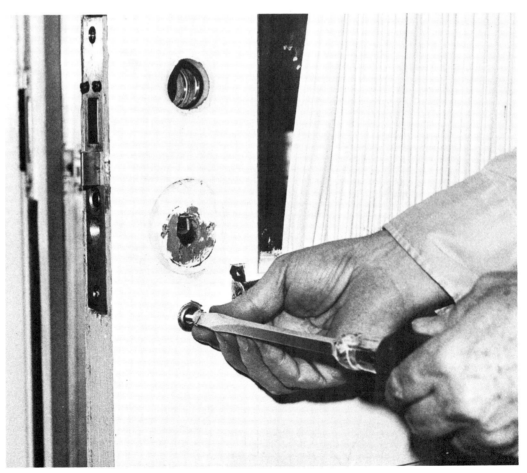

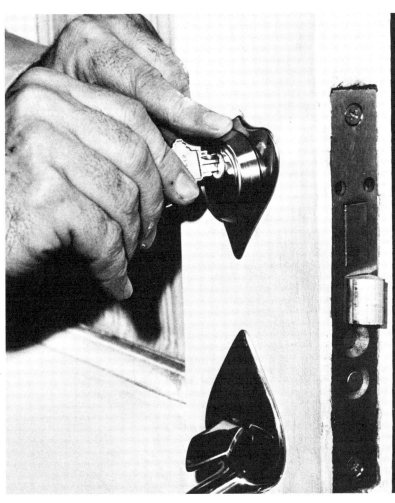

Thread the outside cylinder into the mortise case. This lock has a heart-shaped decorative escutcheon plate through which the cylinder is threaded. In addition, a brass spacer is used to hold the cylinder away from the door surface. This is necessary because there isn't room to thread both the inside and outside cylinders into the door to their full depth (see drawing). Door thicknesses vary, running anywhere from 1⅝ inches thick up to more than 2 inches thick.

Locksmiths solve the problem of door thickness by using a spacer as shown here. The thickness of the spacer is determined by trial and error. Thread both cylinders into the door until they meet in the middle. Back each cylinder out one turn, then use a spacer which adequately fills the space between the face of the door and the front edge of the cylinder.

The spacer used here is a good design. Its edge surrounds the edge of the cylinder. If a burglar tries to clamp a wrench to the cylinder, he will have difficulty turning the cylinder and will be unable to force the lock loose. The spacer will turn but the cylinder will not. (The average lock cylinder is 1⅜ inches deep, but your locksmith has shorter ones to help solve the door thickness problem.)

Side View of Door

Spacer Around Cylinder

Mortise Lock Case

Spacer Around Cylinder

Cylinder

Cylinder

Deadbolt

Spring Latch

Spring Latch
Lock Buttons

Left:
Should you decide to use a decorative plate on the inside of the door, a variety of designs are available. All designs come with a hole for the doorknob, but you must drill the cylinder hole after you have marked where it must be located. Your locksmith or hardware man can do it for you, or you can drill the hole yourself.

Right:
Thread the inside spacer into place using a brass spacer, then tighten the setscrew to hold it.

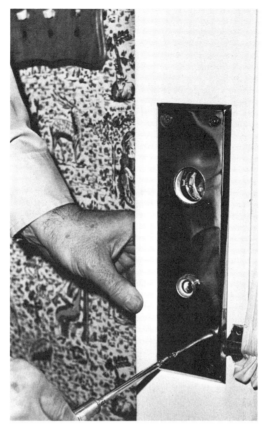
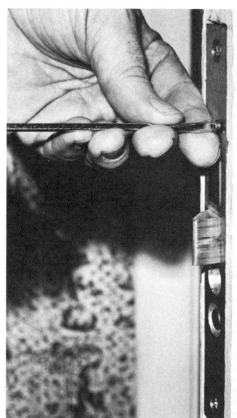

Now insert the lower half of the split doorknob spindle into the doorknob hole. Seat the hooked end in the lock before installing the upper part.

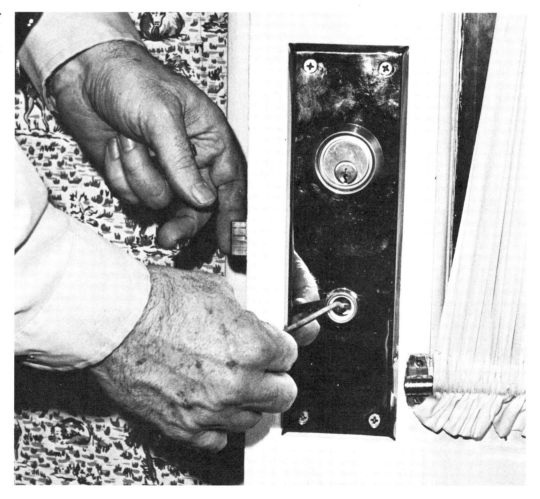

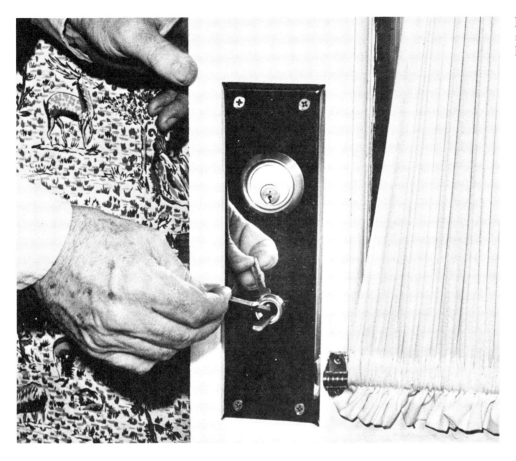

Insert the upper part of the spindle and align it with the lower part.

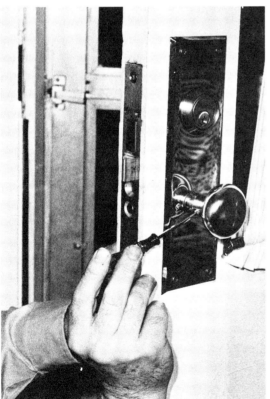

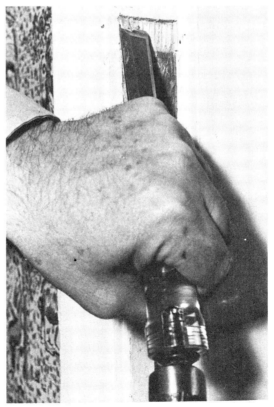

Left:
Thread the doorknob onto the spindles and turn it until it almost touches the plate. Then tighten the setscrew on the shank of the knob to hold the knob firmly in place.

Right:
If the new strike plate is somewhat bigger than the old one, chisel out the jamb to the correct size.

Screw the new strike plate into place, positioning it so that the door, when closed, is held firmly against the doorstop.

CUTTING A MORTISE

Left:
To install a new mortise lock, you must first make the mortise. This is easier to do if you take the door off its hinges. Begin by taping the template which comes with the lock to the edge of the door. Use a nailset or other sharp tool to mark the center of the area to be drilled.

Right:
Using the size of bit indicated on the template, drill on your center marks. The template will tell you how deep to drill the holes.

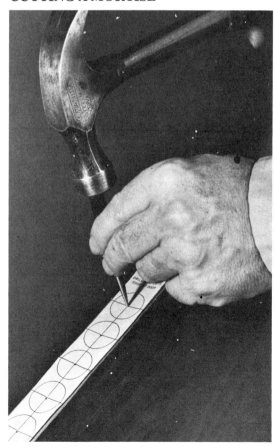

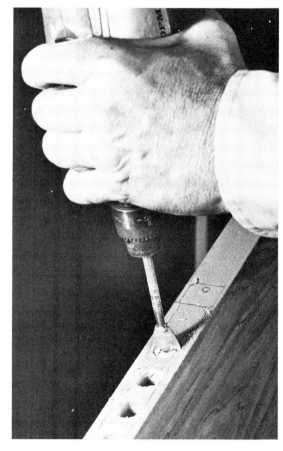

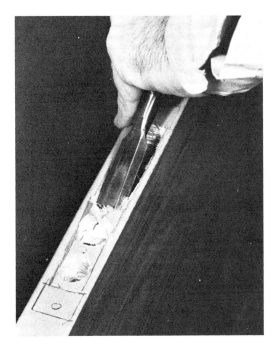

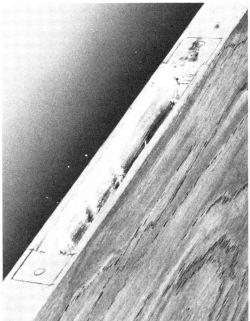

Left:
After drilling, cut out the remaining wood with a sharp chisel. Begin by outlining the area to be cut out with chisel cuts ⅛ inch deep. Then chisel out the wood between the holes up to the outline marks.

Right:
Finish the mortise by chiseling the sides and ends of the mortise to the dimension of your new lock. Chisel out the areas above and below the deep portion of the mortise. These are for the ends of the faceplate, through which it is screwed to the door.

INSTALLING A SEPARATE DEADBOLT

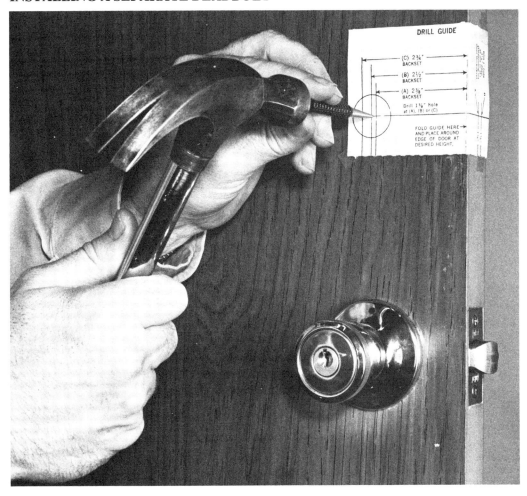

If your door has only a key-in-knob lock, it's a good idea to install a separate deadbolt above it. Begin by taping the template in place and marking the centers of the holes to be drilled in the face and edge of the door.

Left:
Using a drill bit the size called for on the template, drill the hole in the edge of the door.

Right:
Now drill the larger hole in the face of the door. You can use a brace and big bit or a hole saw or hole cutter in your electric drill.

For this next step, you may find it easier to take the door off the hinges. Insert the bolt in the hole and use it as a template to mark the door edge for chiseling.

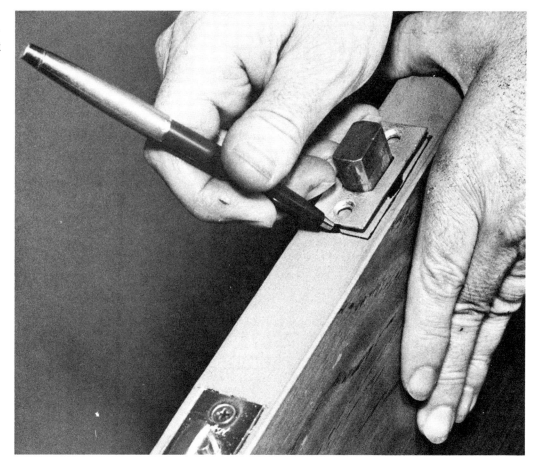

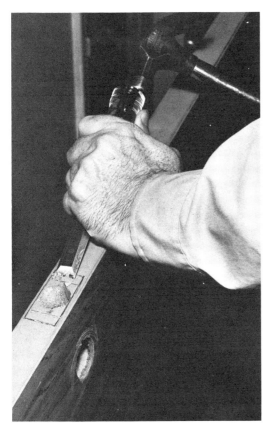

Left:
Outline the area to be chiseled out with ⅛-inch deep chisel cuts. Then make several chisel cuts across the area, ½ inch apart. Begin chiseling at one end, chipping out the wood between the cross cuts. This method gives you good control and eliminates the possibility of chiseling too deep. The cut should be deep enough so that the bolt's faceplate is flush with the door edge.

Right:
If you took the door off the hinges to chisel it, put it back on the hinges now. Insert the bolt in its hole and insert the knob cylinder assembly through the larger hole in the face of the door.

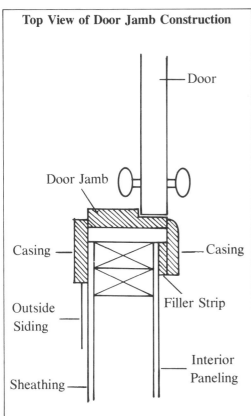

Top View of Door Jamb Construction

Door

Door Jamb

Casing

Casing

Outside
Siding

Filler Strip

Interior
Paneling

Sheathing

Attach the thumb turn by screwing the thumb turn plate to the inside of the door. Install the strike plate in the jamb (see photographs on pages 39, 40), using the template supplied with the lock. Chisel out the wood behind the hole in the strike plate to a depth of about ¾ inch. Also, chisel out the area in which the strike plate is set so that the plate is flush with the wood of the jamb.

Security around Your Windows

Glass windows offer only rudimentary security. A burglar doesn't mind breaking windows to gain entry. The only reason he hesitates is that breaking glass makes an alarming noise: the larger the expanse of glass, the less likely the burglar will be to break it.

The burglar prefers to raise a window to gain entry. If the window is locked, he will try to defeat the lock. If the lock can't be defeated, he may take a chance on breaking or cutting the glass. There are three practical methods of making a window secure: 1) You can install a good lock that prevents the window from opening. 2) You can fasten foil tape which is connected to an alarm system on the window, so that if the window is broken, the alarm is triggered. 3) Or you can put up iron grilles on the outside of your windows so that even if the glass is broken, the burglar can't gain entry.

The method you choose depends on how much security you think you need. In urban areas with a high crime rate, grilles on basement and first floor windows, with locks or alarms on second floor windows, are a good idea. In areas where crime is less prevalent, window locks may be sufficient.

WINDOW LOCKS

Elementary window locks can be purchased for about $.50. They involve a turning latch mounted on the lower sash, which engages a flange mounted on the lower part of the upper sash. When the latch and flange are engaged, the window can't be raised. This type of lock can be opened easily by an experienced burglar forcing a long knife blade up between the window sash to release the lock.

A better version of this type window lock permits you to lock the turning latch with a key. This version cannot be opened with a knife, nor can it be opened if the window is broken or cut.

Ventilation locks are mounted on the lower sash and locked with a key. This style lock permits the window to be opened part way for ventilation and then locked in that position.

Casement windows, windows mounted on hinges to open outward, have locks at the top and bottom of the windows and can't be opened by a burglar from the outside unless he breaks the glass, in which case the casement window offers no problem for the burglar. A good way to lock casement windows is to remove the handles from the operating cranks. Without the handles, the windows are immobilized.

Louvered windows are locked in the same manner as casement windows. However, a burglar can't enter through them unless he smashes the louvers and risks making a great deal of noise.

Some basement windows, notably metal-framed windows, have built-in hasps on their latches, into which padlocks can be inserted. A window that doesn't have such an arrangement can be locked by driving a screw into the wood or masonry near the edge of the window. The screw head blocks the window from opening.

WINDOW BARS

Barred windows are more secure, but they present some problems. The first problem is one of appearance. Ordinary iron bars or heavy mesh across the window tends to make your home look like a jail. You can solve this problem by shopping for decorative wrought iron grilles, which are available in many interesting designs. These can actually enhance the appearance of a house, but they tend to be expensive.

The second problem is one of safety. The bars that keep a burglar out also lock the occupants of the house in. In the event of a fire, you may need to get out through a window; the bars could prevent your escape. For this reason, building codes prohibit the use of bars unless they are hinged or have some other means of being opened from the inside. Since these grilles are locked, and a lock can be forced or picked, they aren't as secure as they might appear to be.

Another problem with bars is that they give the daring burglar a perfect handhold or place to put a pry bar. If he can work for a few minutes without detection, he stands a pretty good chance of being able to pull the bars from the window. Use bars to increase your security, but don't regard them as foolproof protection.

PLASTIC WINDOWS

Acrylic plastic sheets, as thick or thicker than ordinary window glass, have been on the market for a long time and are now widely used as an alternative to glass. For a long time the plastic sheets were much more expensive than glass; the price differential is now less.

Plastic is hard to break and therefore more secure than glass. Because plastic doesn't shatter, and because it is safer than glass for many uses, a number of state building codes require plastic window panes in all doors, storm doors, and even in windows in the vicinity of doors.

Plastic windows don't transmit heat or cold as readily as glass, and therefore offer some value as insulators. But plastic is softer and can be scratched easily; you must take care when handling it or live with scratches on your windows.

WINDOW SECURITY PROBLEMS

Second floor windows are particularly vulnerable when they open over a roof, near a tree, or onto a porch, balcony, or sundeck. Second floor windows should have locks as secure as those used on the first floor.

It is easy to forget to lock windows. If your house is air conditioned, of course, you can lock the windows and forget them for long periods of time. But if you don't have a cooling system, you probably open the windows frequently for ventilation. Running through the house to lock all of them may prove too big a job. Unfortunately, the price of security is eternal vigilance.

SLIDING GLASS DOORS

The locks which come on the average sliding glass door are incredibly easy to defeat; most burglars hardly regard them as locks. You can buy any of several types of locks which fit into the track at the bottom of the window, and these do a much better job than the simple latch near the handle. You can also buy an aluminum bar to fit between one of the doors and the jamb. The bar makes it impossible to open the door from the outside. For an equally effective, virtually invisible, no-cost lock, you can cut a broomstick to the proper length and drop it into the track when the glass doors are closed.

Sliding glass doors can be broken, but there is so much glass in them that the burglar who wants to remain anonymous will probably leave such doors alone. A more daring thief or a drug addict might not be so cautious.

From a security standpoint, this home is in good shape. The shrubs have been trimmed so they offer no screen behind which a burglar could work on entry.

Left:
These shutters are ornamental, but the old fashioned shutters which can be closed and locked are making a comeback in some areas, chiefly because of the additional security they offer.

Right:
The three windows which open over a roof on the second floor of this house offer easy access to a burglar; they should be locked.

This type window lock is the simplest, most inexpensive one and can be installed in less than 5 minutes. It can, however, be forced open by an intruder who knows how to drive a knife blade up between the upper and lower sashes.

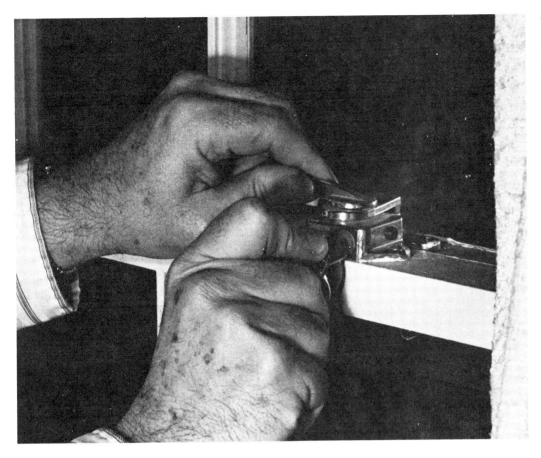

Once this latch has been turned to the locked position, and the key has been turned to lock it into that position, a knife blade can't open the window.

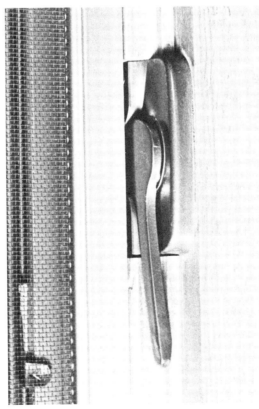

Left:
One good way to secure a casement window is to remove the handle from the cranking mechanism. The window can't be operated without the crank.

Right:
This lock at the top of a casement window can't be defeated by a burglar from the outside, but is easily opened if the window is broken.

A ventilating lock permits a window to be locked with a key in the closed position and in one open position.

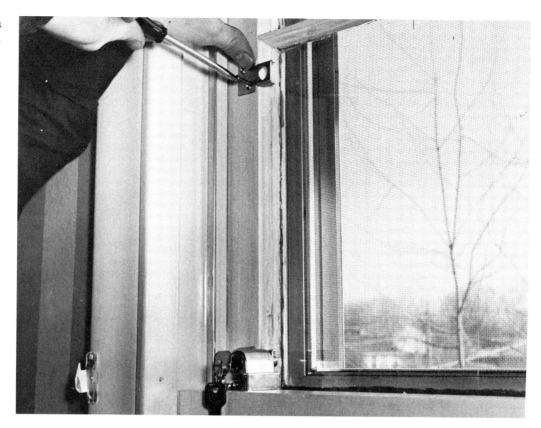

You need only a nail and a drill to make a fairly effective window lock. Simply drill through both sashes and insert a long nail. A second hole about 8 inches higher on the upper sash would permit you to lock the window open for ventilation.

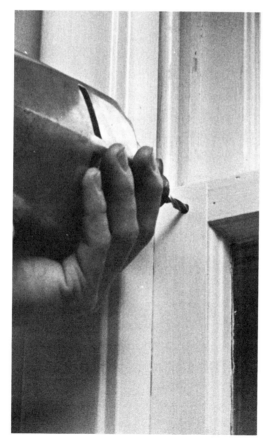

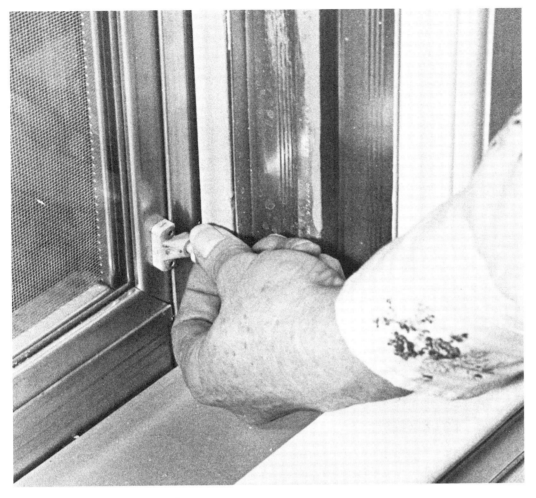

Storm windows and screens now come with latches. The latch on the screen, which can be slit with a penknife, doesn't mean much, but the window latch does make a difference when the window is in position. The burglar must jimmy the storm window to get at the regular window. Don't count on storm windows for security, only as a deterrent to intruders.

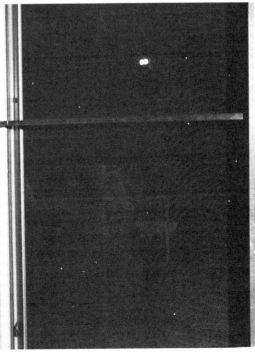

Secure a sliding glass door with either a broomstick cut to the proper length and dropped into the track or an aluminum bar. Both devices prevent the door from moving.

This grille covers a window well and a basement window. It is practical, but not pretty.

Left:
The ornamental grille on this basement window is both effective and attractive. It is hinged to swing out in the event of an emergency.

Right:
This high first floor is protected by three-quarter grilles on the windows. Grilles for use outside of casement windows are similar to these grilles but must be extended far enough from the window to permit the windows to swing open.

Lighting for Security

Experts say that good exterior lighting is a strong deterrent to burglars and prowlers. This may seem strange in view of the fact that more than half of all burglaries take place in broad daylight, but the experts have some statistics on their side. Businesses and homes which have been victimized frequently have had much less trouble after exterior lights have been installed.

Lighting in and around your home can be important not only to security but also to safety; too many home accidents can be traced to poor lighting.

EXTERIOR LIGHTING

The ideal lighting for a home centered on a lot and somewhat removed from the homes on either side is a system which can bathe the entire house in light. This type of lighting usually can be achieved with a dozen or so floodlights mounted in clusters of two or three.

Easy and inexpensive to install, floodlights are most often mounted on the eaves at the corners of the house. One cluster of lights at a corner can provide light for at least a portion of two walls. Additional lighting may be installed at ground level and directed toward the house.

Lights that are installed in the ground create some safety problems. They are accessible to children, and people unaware of their location may trip over them. If possible, locate ground lights in planted areas, where they are both concealed and out of the general traffic pattern.

If there is an electric utility pole on your property or on an easement adjacent to your lot, the electric company will often mount a light similar to those used in street lighting for an installation fee plus a small monthly charge. These lights illuminate an area of a thousand square feet or more and will automatically turn on at dusk and off at dawn.

Installing Eave Light

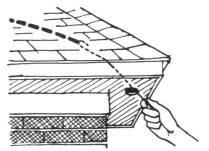

Drill a 1-inch hole in the soffit, positioning it where you wish the floodlights to appear. Connect one end of the cable to a grounded junction box inside the house. Pass the cable through the hole to the outside.

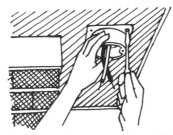

Secure the outside end of the cable to a special weatherproof outdoor box with locknut. Leave about 4 inches of cable hanging for connecting the light fixtures.

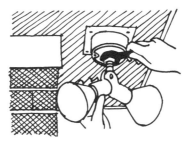

Connect the cable white wire to the fixture white wire; connect the cable black wire to the fixture black wire. Secure the fixture assembly with the bolts provided.

When an entire home is not lighted, provide illumination at least for the vulnerable places. These include the front and back entranceways, passageways or walks beside the house, the front of the garage (whether it is attached to the house or separate), and ground floor windows.

Outdoor lighting designed for better security should be installed so that most of the lights can be controlled from one centrally located panel. For convenience many systems locate this panel in the master bedroom.

Entrance lighting should be controlled separately by switches just inside the door. Entranceway lights should be bright enough to permit you to easily identify anyone coming to your home.

Exterior lights can be wired into any burglar alarm system so that when the alarm is tripped off, the lights suddenly flash on. The sudden noise of the alarm, plus the bright lights, will scare away all but the most dedicated burglars.

GROUND LIGHTS

A plastic-covered cable has been developed for use in underground wiring installations. This type of wiring is less expensive and easier to install than conduit wiring, which has been standard for

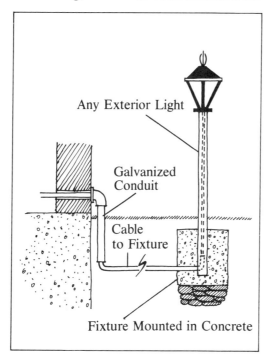

Any Exterior Light

Galvanized Conduit

Cable to Fixture

Fixture Mounted in Concrete

years. The plastic cable is water-proof and resists acids and alkali. Whether or not you can use this cable for the installation of ground-level security lights depends on your local electrical code. Some codes demand that only conduit or lead-sheathed cable be used for underground wiring.

Keep in mind that all electrical installations must conform to the National Electric Code or your local electrical code, whichever is most stringent. All installations must be made by a licensed electrician or inspected and approved by your community's Building or Electrical Department after completion. An uninspected electrical installation may void your insurance in the event of an electrically caused fire. In some communities, you may need a permit before making any electrical installations.

Use only fixtures made for outdoor installation. In addition to floodlights, these include decorative garden lights and porch and post lanterns. Portable outdoor lights are also available. Portable lights are mounted on spikes, which may be driven into the ground, and are plugged into nearby receptacles. Such receptacles must be made especially for outdoor use.

In planning outdoor illumination, it is best to have the system on a separate circuit—fused separately from the other home circuits. This should apply whether you use underground wiring or mount the lights on the eaves of your home.

LIGHTING FOR SAFETY

Effective lighting may help prevent accidents. Inadequately or unevenly lighted stairways, particularly a basement stairway, are responsible for many serious falls. Too often basement and attic storage areas are illuminated by a single, poorly placed, bare bulb which fails to light up potential hazards.

One common lighting safety problem is a room which does not have a light switch at the door. A person entering such a room must grope to find a lamp to turn on. There is a good chance he will trip over something and become one of the National Safety Council's statistics.

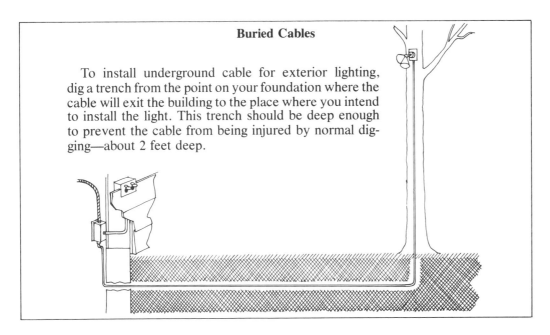

Buried Cables

To install underground cable for exterior lighting, dig a trench from the point on your foundation where the cable will exit the building to the place where you intend to install the light. This trench should be deep enough to prevent the cable from being injured by normal digging—about 2 feet deep.

In apartment buildings, hallways, stairwells, basement and laundry areas, and the front lobbies must be brightly lighted for security as well as safety. If these areas are not bright enough in your building, discuss the problem with your landlord. Remind him that accidents on the property because of inadequate lighting can raise insurance problems.

AUTOMATIC GARAGE DOORS

An automatic garage door, operated by a pushbutton from your car, is a good security measure. You can open the garage door as you approach the house and drive into a well-lighted garage, avoiding any prowlers who might be lurking outside of the house. The lights switch on automatically as the garage doors rise.

When shopping for an automatic garage door, check for special safety features in addition to automatic lighting: a security switch that cuts off the transmitter, so that the doors can be opened only from the receiver inside of the garage or by key; automatic reversing mechanisms that cause the doors to go back up if they encounter any obstacles, such as a bicycle, on the way down; and a light-delay system, which turns the garage lights off several minutes after you pull in, giving you enough time to leave the car and enter the house.

You should be able to operate the doors manually in the event of a power failure. The automatic reversing feature should shut off during the last few inches as the door travels downward, so that any ice or snow which has accumulated under the door won't send the door back up again.

This house was lighted for security reasons. Lights mounted on the eaves are used to spotlight vulnerable areas at windows and to put extra light on the entranceway.

Bushes could conceal a burglar attempting to enter via the windows. A spotlight on the eaves will expose him as he works.

This home was lighted for decorative reasons and with outdoor living in mind, but the lights also serve a security purpose.

A cluster of floodlights located under the eaves at the peak of the house can be used to illuminate a large section of the yard.

Sidelights at the front door are attractive but may not give sufficient light to enable you to easily identify visitors at night.

Left:
The area directly in front of the garage door should be well lighted. The lights could be tied into the automatic garage door circuit to switch on as you approach the door.

Right:
The overhead light provides the needed additional illumination for this front door. The peephole is hidden in the decorative door knocker.

Left:
A yard light, whether gas or electric, improves the appearance of your property and provides some exterior illumination, but it should be supplemented by floodlights around the house for the best security.

Right:
Portable floodlight units can be plugged into outdoor electric wall outlets. If you install outdoor outlets, be sure to purchase only weatherproof equipment designed specifically for outdoor use.

The automatic garage door, opened by a button-controlled radio transmitter from your car, is a good security measure as well as a convenience. The lights in the garage switch on automatically as the door raises and shut off automatically several minutes later, giving you enough time to leave the car and enter the house.

Alarm Systems

Burglar and fire alarm systems perform some very necessary security services that you can't get through any other means. The greatest benefit you get from these systems is an easier mind. But having them around can also be a great annoyance.

It is easy to accidentally trip off the alarm system. You must be conscious of the system at all times and know whether it is on or off. People who have a new alarm system in their homes are likely to trip the alarm half a dozen times in the first few weeks. As one of my friends says, "It's like having another member of the family to worry about."

False alarms are funny the first time or two. After that, you may become the neighborhood nuisance. Not too many people enjoy listening to alarms screaming at 2 o'clock in the morning. Police in many areas have been swamped with false alarms and are now charging $25 for each unnecessary call.

HAVING AN ALARM SYSTEM INSTALLED

Should you consider having an alarm system installed? If you have unusually valuable items, a burglar alarm system can protect these possessions better than any other security measure. At the same time, an alarm system is an added responsibility; you must be prepared to invest not only cash, but also time and patience in making the system operate effectively for your home.

If you have pets, be particularly careful when considering what type of alarm system to install. Pets walking through the house will set off some types of alarm—pressure-sensitive mats, ul-trasonic motion detectors, and photo-electric cell beams. Your alarm system must be designed with your pets in mind or you will have alarms sounding at all hours.

There is no such thing as a packaged burglar alarm system that is satisfactory. Each system must be tailored for the needs of your house. You need some types of protection but may not need others. You may wish a certain kind of protection even though you don't need it. For some, minimum protection is enough; others want the whole deluxe system.

The cost of a professionally installed alarm system varies with the equipment used. A minimum security system might cost in the area of $600 or so, installed. For a complete, elaborate system utilizing very sophisticated equipment, the cost might run as high as $4,500, installed.

Many alarm systems may be leased rather than purchased. Most reputable alarm dealers have systems available for lease as well as for sale.

When you lease, there is an initial one-time installation charge. After this initial charge, you pay a monthly fee which covers any servicing that is necessary to maintain the equipment. Leasing a minimum security system might cost you an initial $300 to $400 and monthly fees of $10 to $20. The charge varies from system to system because every alarm system is custom-tailored to the needs of the particular house.

Leasing a very elaborate system may involve an initial charge of $1,000 and monthly fees ranging from $30 to as much as $80. If your alarm system is tied to the central desk of a private monitoring service, you pay a fee of $10 to $12 per month.

Shop carefully when looking for someone to install your alarm system. Don't buy alarm equipment or installation services from a door-to-door salesman. To get dealer recommendations check with the Better Business Bureau, local police, and friends who already have satisfactory alarm systems.

You should be concerned with much more than just getting your money's worth; when you contract with an alarm installer, you literally place the security of your home in his hands. There have been many instances where this month's alarm installer turned out to be next month's burglar. Who would know better how to defeat the system?

As a final check, ask the installer for references and talk to the people whose homes he has serviced.

TYPES OF EQUIPMENT

An alarm system consists of a number of components, mostly sensing units or switches, tied together into a system. There are two basic types of systems: the wired and the wireless. All components in the wired system are tied together by connecting wires. In the wireless system, the sensors transmit information to the central control panel by radio.

Experts say the wireless system is difficult to control because the radio sig-

nals can be interfered with. You have no way of knowing when the transmitters are working or when batteries are low. For these reasons, experts generally recommend wired systems.

Burglar alarm systems operate in varied ways. Switches, usually of the magnetic type, on doors and windows trip the alarm when either is opened. Foil tape on a window tied into the system sets off the alarm when the window is broken. Ultrasonic motion detectors survey a broad area of a room and detect anyone walking in that area. Pressure-sensitive mats under rugs sound the alarm when anyone walks on the rug. Automatic telephone dialers installed in the system are programmed to dial any number, including the police station, and deliver a prerecorded message.

Fire detectors consist mainly of heat and smoke sensors. Heat sensors are set to sound an alarm when the temperature around them reaches 135°. But by the time a fire has raised the air temperature to 135°, the fire has progressed pretty far, so a heat sensor warning is late.

Smoke sensors sound an alarm when the particulate matter in the air exceeds 2 to 4 percent. A smoke sensor is preferred for warning a family of fire because it sounds the alarm much earlier than the heat sensor and allows more time for escape.

Alarm devices consist of sirens, screamers, or loud bells. Experts believe the screamer is best; sirens may burn out after some use, and bells cannot be heard as far away as screamers.

In some areas, alarm systems can be connected to the police or fire station switchboard. Where this arrangement is prohibited, the system may, instead, be connected to the central alarm board of a private monitoring agency, which will answer the alarm and notify the local police. Some homeowners are content simply to have the alarm sound off without it having any connection to security desks.

INSURANCE DISCOUNTS

Insurance companies have experienced increased costs as a result of the

If you have an alarm system installed, the installer will post warning decals similar to this one around your property. Would-be burglars tend to avoid houses where they know a good alarm system is in operation.

rising number of burglaries. To cut these costs, they want to encourage the use of alarm systems; many insurance companies are offering premium discounts for customers who install burglar alarm systems.

The discount varies from company to company, and may not be offered to those homeowners who have already experienced a costly burglary. The discount may be 2 percent for the installation of a satisfactory, self-contained system; 5 percent if the system is tied into a police switchboard; and 10 percent if the system is tied into a private central alarm desk.

Check with your insurance agent for his company's latest information concerning premium discounts for homes with alarm devices.

Although not part of an alarm system, a good intercom system is an addition to the safety and security of your home. You can question persons at the front door from the central station or monitor the baby in the nursery while you are in the kitchen. Most intercom systems consist of a central station, a unit at the front door, and units in other rooms such as bedrooms, the den, and the basement workshop.

Left:
This smoke sensor, mounted in a hallway leading to the bedrooms, will set off an alarm if the concentration of particles in the air exceeds 2 percent. It gives an early warning of fire in the home.

Right:
An ultrasonic motion detector, mounted on a beam in the ceiling of the living room, can detect the slightest motion in the wide area it surveys. A cat walking across the area would trigger the alarm. Experts consider the ultrasonic motion detector to be one of the most effective security measures available to homeowners.

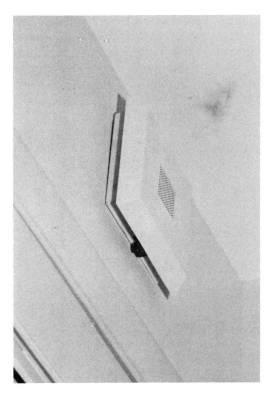

This type alarm system employs a bell located in a locked box outside of the house. The homeowner can turn the system on and off with a special key inserted into the metal plate on the wall.

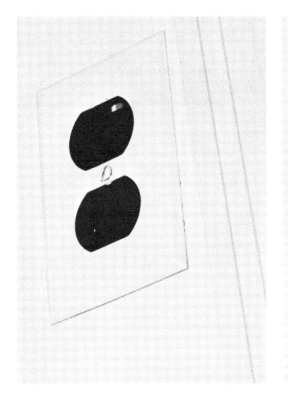

Left:
Though this unit in the wall just above the baseboard looks like an electric wall outlet, it is actually one unit in an infrared photoelectric cell alarm system. A burglar walking down a hall surveyed by this unit would set off the alarm. Normal lighting does not affect this system.

Right:
The switch on this doorframe sets off an alarm when the door is opened.

This is the panel for turning an alarm system on and off. It is located in the garage so that it can be operated on the way to and from the car.

Installing Your Own Alarm System

Should you choose to install your own alarm devices or to develop a personalized alarm system, you will find that the various components can be purchased from national mail order houses, radio supply stores, and local hardware and home centers. Some of the components are even available in kit form. The units generally available include the following components:

Magnetic contact switches used on doors and windows to sound an alarm in the event either is opened.

Foil tape and foil block connectors applied to windows to set off the alarm system if a window is broken.

Heat sensors which set off the alarm when the air in the vicinity of the sensor reaches 135°.

Smoke sensors which sense the products of combustion in the air and trip the alarm when the concentration of particles exceeds 2 percent. These units give the earliest warning of fire in your house.

Ultrasonic motion detectors, compact little boxes which monitor the space in front of them and trip the alarm if anything in that area moves. Don't install one of these if you have a pet.

Alarm bells, sirens, and screamers, the loud voices of the alarm system. Experts generally favor the screamers. Sirens, they say, are apt to burn out, and bells don't attract as much attention.

Panic buttons, resembling ordinary doorbell buttons, wired into the system and placed at strategic points like the front and back doors and in the master bedroom. When you hit them, they activate the alarm.

Master control panels, the central units around which an alarm system must be assembled.

POWER FOR THE ALARM SYSTEM

Alarm systems operate on low-voltage current, like doorbells do, and draw their power either from batteries or from house current which has been reduced by a transformer (again, like a doorbell). Many systems are set up with rechargeable batteries and with trickle chargers connected to the batteries to keep them fresh and alive. The charger operates off standard house current.

Keep in mind that your local electrical code has regulations regarding the installation of burglar and fire alarms as well as certain specifications for the kind of equipment which may be used. Before attempting to install a system, and before purchasing any components, check with the local authorities and learn these limitations. Also, check to see what inspection is required after the work has been completed.

If you do install a system, remember that burglars know about alarm systems; in casing a house, they look for ways to defeat alarms. One of the things they look for is the wires which connect the elements of the system. To make your system effective, you must hide the wiring. Conceal all necessary wires behind baseboards and other moldings; never let them run in the open, especially not within view of a window.

DESIGNING THE ALARM SYSTEM

Where do you need security? When designing an alarm system, look around and decide where you need the extra protection and where you don't need it. Even the simplest alarm system should include switches on the front door and any other door opening to the outside.

The second most obvious place to protect would be ground floor windows, especially if they are concealed by large shrubs or located on the back of the house. These windows should be equipped with magnetic switches which will set off an alarm when someone opens the window.

If you wish to protect valuable posses-

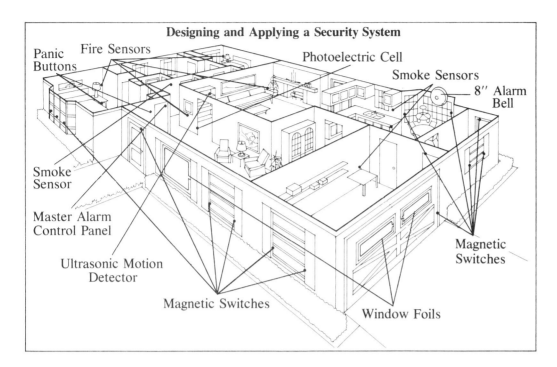

Designing and Applying a Security System

Panic Buttons

Fire Sensors

Photoelectric Cell

Smoke Sensors

8" Alarm Bell

Smoke Sensor

Master Alarm Control Panel

Ultrasonic Motion Detector

Magnetic Switches

Magnetic Switches

Window Foils

sions which are stored or displayed in one particular room, consider using an ultrasonic motion detector in this room. But keep in mind that by the time a burglar is detected by this sensor, he is already in the house. Concentrate your efforts on safeguarding the perimeter of the house first.

Foil tape applied to the windows will trip the alarm when the windows are broken, but many people object to the appearance of the tape. Tape is commonly used in business alarm systems, but not as often in home systems, although it does help provide security for vulnerable windows—especially big ones.

Panic buttons are a good idea for any alarm system. In the event that an intruder should push his way through the front door, the person at the door can hit the panic button and sound the alarm. A panic button is often installed in the master bedroom.

Fire and smoke detectors are good protection. Smoke sensors, although more expensive, offer the best protection. These units are installed on or near the ceiling and should be centrally located. More elaborate systems might have both a fire and a smoke detector in every room. One good place to install such a

unit would be at the top of the stairway to the second floor. In a single-story house, a sensor should be located in the hall leading to the bedroom area.

Make a plan of your home and draw in the types of equipment you need. Then shop around. Some alarm systems are of low quality and price, and while these systems might be satisfactory for a while, they are not likely to be very dependable in the long run. Invest in high quality equipment.

WIRING THE ALARM SYSTEM

Check the wiring diagram in this chapter to get a general indication of how an alarm system is wired. Also check the instruction sheets which come with each piece of equipment.

There are two types of sensors or switches included in an alarm system. One type is normally open while the other type is normally closed. A doorbell push button is normally open; you push it closed to complete the circuit. Sensors which are normally open are closed by the action they monitor. A heat sensor, for example, is closed by rising heat.

A typical, normally closed switch is the magnetic switch mounted on a door or window. As long as the two magnets are together, as they are when the door

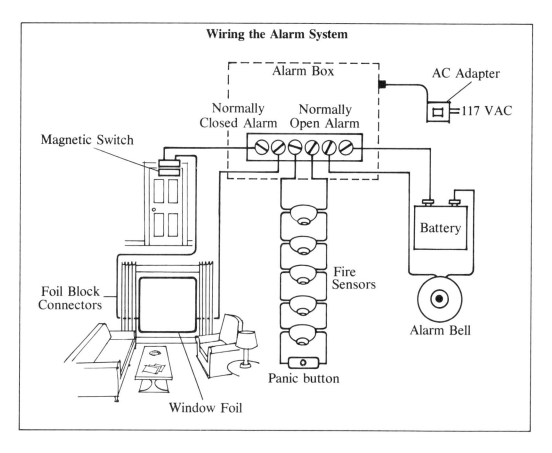

Wiring the Alarm System

and the jamb are in contact with each other, the switches are closed. When the door is opened, the switch is opened and the alarm sounds.

Keep this rule in mind: normally closed sensors or switches must be wired in series. Normally open sensors and switches must be wired in parallel. These two wiring methods are made clear in the diagrams which accompany the alarm system. The package in which the switch or sensor comes will tell you whether it is normally open or normally closed.

MASTER CONTROL PANEL

The heart of any alarm system is the master control panel which is available for a cost as low as $30. Better quality units cost quite a bit more. Master control panels should be mounted out of sight, such as on the wall of a closet, but they must be easy to reach since they are used to turn on and off the entire system.

There are contact screws in the panel to which each of the sensor circuits is connected. There is also an instant-delay switch. This switch enables you to acti-

vate the system instantly or to delay it for 30 seconds. This 30-second delay gives you time to leave the house before the alarm system goes into operation. Don't be late getting out or the alarm will go off.

Master control panels also have facilities for connecting an AC adapter. The alarm system normally operates on battery power. When the AC adapter is attached, it supplies a low voltage reduced from household current and operates the system. The battery then becomes a standby source of power and cuts in only when the main power source fails or is turned off. Most systems operate on 9 volt lantern batteries.

As a rule, do-it-yourself alarm systems do not have the same level of reliability as professionally installed alarm systems have. For this reason, you shouldn't be tempted to spend too much money on such a system unless electronics is your hobby and you can do the work of an electrician. If your plan shows that you will spend several hundred dollars, you would be wiser to call in a professional.

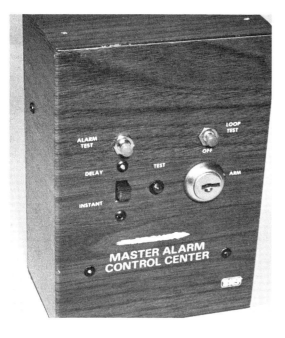

Left:
This typical, inexpensive, master alarm control box comes with a key with which you turn the alarm system on and off; it permits you to test the system and to activate it either instantly or with a 30-second delay.

Right:
Large and small alarm bells are available. The large bell serves as part of a burglar alarm system and is mounted outside the home in a locked metal cabinet. The smaller bell is usually used in fire alarm systems and is located inside the home to arouse occupants.

The electronic screamer produces plenty of noise and is preferred by most alarm experts.

Photoelectric cells trip the alarm when anyone breaks the beam sent from one unit to the other. This system is used especially to protect hallways.

Installing Your Own Alarm System   65

The ultrasonic motion detector comes in a neat, unobtrusive package. Some are made to look like books and can be placed on library shelves. These units detect and set off an alarm when any motion takes place in front of them.

Left:
Magnetic switches are used to detect the opening of a door or window. If the two parts of the switch are separated, the alarm sounds.

Right:
A back view of a heat sensor shows how the unit is wired in parallel.

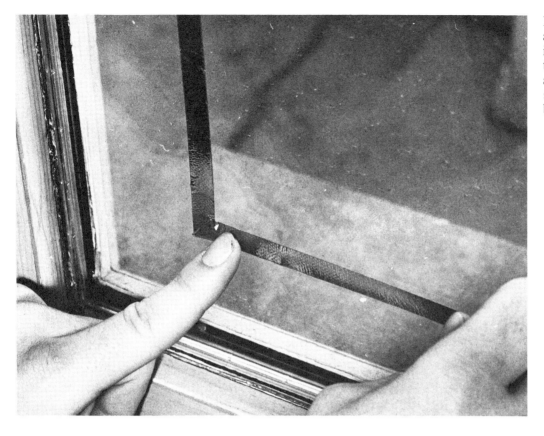

Foil tape is self-adhesive and should be applied 2 inches in from the edge of the window. The tape is applied in a continuous strip; corners are formed by bending and folding it.

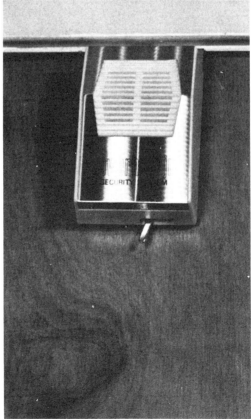

Left:
Each end of the foil tape on a window is connected to a foil block connector at the edge of the window. The block connector is wired to the main alarm system.

Right:
This door alarm is a typical battery-powered, self-contained alarm unit. It clips to the top of the door, and when the door is opened, the alarm sounds. Alarms such as this provide some security but are limited in value since the alarm usually cannot be heard for any great distance.

Apartment Security

Safety and security measures for people who live in apartments are in most respects the same as those for homeowners but with one significant difference: the apartment dweller doesn't own the dwelling and therefore cannot make changes in it without the consent of the landlord.

Cooperation between the landlord and the tenants—and among the tenants themselves—is essential if good apartment security is to be achieved. The landlord and the tenants together have the responsibility of identifying security problems and of working out sensible solutions.

The vulnerable sites in an apartment include ground level windows, windows which look out onto a fire escape or balcony, lobbies, elevators, laundry and storage areas, halls, and the exterior doors of each apartment.

The problems in these areas can be minimized, if not eliminated, by effective lighting, sturdy, high-quality door and window hardware, strict control of apartment keys, and perpetual maintenance of all security equipment, such as annunciators.

Part of the problem of apartment security is the expense. Another problem is the fact that too often every tenant has a different idea about exactly what should be done to achieve security, and no single program is ever effectively worked out or enforced.

The only sensible answer to apartment security problems is a cooperative effort, involving both the tenants and the building management. Develop a program that all can agree to and that will actually increase security. Either management or a group of tenants can initiate this effort but until someone does, security will remain a problem.

Carry out a small survey of your own apartment. The door should be solid wood and should have two locks, one of which is a deadbolt or a vertical bolt. The windows should have locks, preferably with keys, and should have grilles or heavy wire mesh on the outside if they can be reached from the fire escape or from another building. If you can employ these security measures, you will be reasonably safe within your own apartment; your security as you enter the main building and travel to your apartment must be worked out with the other tenants and the landlord.

Check your habits. Be careful around laundry and storage areas; these are semipublic and often open to almost anyone who wants to come in. Don't enter these areas alone unless they are well lit. Don't enter if there is a total stranger already inside. The same rules apply to riding in elevators.

If you come home and find that the lights in the lobby are out or are much dimmer than they were the previous night, don't enter the lobby or at least don't enter alone. Unscrewing light bulbs to create a dark lobby is an old and favorite trick of intruders.

Treat your front door as if it opened directly onto the street. Don't open it unless you are sure just who is on the other side. Keep the chain on the door when you do open it.

Don't enter dim passageways between buildings. Don't treat the back porch and back stairway as if they had the same security as your individual apartment unit; these places are either public or semipublic, and almost anyone has access to them.

Many people have lived in apartment

buildings for years and seldom or never have had security problems, although there may have been problems all around them. Such people don't have serious security problems because they take serious precautions and literally make these precautions a part of their daily routines.

In modern high-rise apartment buildings, security is often a part of the design. This lobby is laid out with both appearance and security in mind, but even with the improvements made in security measures over those in older apartment buildings, security remains a problem solved only by cooperation between management and tenants.

In apartments with individual outside entrances, the need for making the apartment secure tends to fall back on the individual tenant; landlord-tenant cooperation becomes less important.

Laundry areas have been the scene of too many crimes. They should be well lighted, and their use should be restricted to certain hours. Don't enter such areas if there is a stranger around, and don't remain in the room alone, particularly at night.

This outside sheltered stairway is fairly well lighted, but the turns in the stairway are a good place for a prowler to hide. Don't walk in areas like this alone.

This hall offers good security. You can see the entire length of it, and there are no alcoves or nooks in which anyone can hide. Lighting could be better, but at least you can see the entire hall from this end.

Left:
This apartment building has a fire alarm system with a bell mounted in the hallway on each floor. Tenants are instructed about what to do if the bell rings.

Right:
This smoke sensor is centrally located in the hall of the apartment building.

Fight Fires before They Flare

Almost every residential fire could be prevented. National fire statistics reflect the causes of many fires, and a glance at the charts at the end of Chapter I will tell you that with preparation and awareness, most of these fires wouldn't have occurred.

Minimize the hazard of fire around your home by attacking the problem from two directions: 1) eliminate fire causes, and 2) minimize damage and injury if a fire should break out in spite of your preventive effort.

The majority of residential fires can be traced back to one of the following causes: cigarette smoking, electrical problems, children playing with matches, cooking, faulty heating equipment, misuse of flammable chemicals.

Smoking is the leading cause of home fires, chiefly because smokers often doze off while smoking in bed or on upholstered furniture. Poorly designed ashtrays which allow lighted cigarettes to fall to the carpet and ashtrays that are emptied into waste baskets while cigarettes are still hot contribute to the high number of home fires.

If there are smokers in your home, you must make and enforce strict rules in order to minimize the chance of fire. Get rid of ashtrays that don't hold cigarettes properly; always empty ashtrays into the toilet, not a waste basket; enforce the rule: no smoking permitted in any bedroom. These may seem like difficult rules to live with, but remember that nearly 300 residential fires each day are caused by careless smoking habits.

Electrical problems may be tougher to fight than bad smoking habits. Begin to ensure electrical safety by discarding all extension cords that are frayed, worn, split, or otherwise in bad condition. Have all appliances in good repair. Don't insert more than two plugs into any one wall outlet; don't plug two appliances which use heat into a single wall outlet.

If you blow fuses frequently, beware. The fuse box is trying to tell you that you are overloading the circuits or that there is other trouble. Call an electrician and have him look over your electrical system. You probably need two or three more circuits.

Fire fascinates children; they'll play with matches or cigarette lighters if they get the opportunity. Put these items away. Even more important, teach your children at an early age that fire is painful and that it is dangerous.

Most kitchen fires are the result of mishandling grease or cooking oils, and such fires spread quickly if there is an accumulation of grease in the hood over the range. Pretty kitchen curtains often help fire spread, too.

Clean the hood and chute behind it on a regular basis, using a grease-cutting detergent. Remove any curtains near the oven or range; don't store cooking fats near the range; and keep a fire extinguisher of the type designed for controlling grease fires handy in the kitchen area.

The best way to avoid fires from faulty heating equipment is to have the equipment checked and adjusted regularly by a professional furnace man. By maintaining your furnace, you'll get more efficient heat, your furnace will last longer, and the danger of fire will be reduced. Check chimneys for any soot build-up. Chimneys and flues should be cleaned at regular intervals or they become fire hazards.

The number of chemical fires in U. S. homes is greater now than it used to be, apparently because more powerful chemicals are used these days. Chemicals around the home present three main fire problems: 1) the storage of chemical-soaked rags, which often ignite later through spontaneous combustion; 2) improper storage of containers which hold chemicals; 3) and the misuse of these chemicals, which often are highly volatile and quickly fill the air with dangerous fumes.

If you use any volatile chemical in a closed room—gasoline or lacquer thinner, for example—the fumes rapidly increase in concentration until the air of the room actually becomes combustible. At that point, any raw flame can set off a fire. This could be the pilot light on a hot water heater, a match used to light a cigarette, or even a small spark caused when you switch on the lights.

You should always use chemicals in a well-ventilated area; never store oily or chemical-soaked cloths. (Dust mops soaked with oil have caused a good many fires because they were stored in airless broom closets.) Always store chemicals in tightly sealed containers. Don't store containers of chemicals near a heat source; in fact, avoid storing them in the house at all if possible.

PREPARING FOR A FIRE

Even if you take every precaution to prevent fires, they can still happen. Your second line of defense should be to prepare for that eventuality:

1. *Install a fire alarm system, employing smoke sensors.* (See the chapter on alarm systems.)

2. *Install fire extinguishers in your home.* (See latter part of this chapter.)

3. *Have fire drills that involve your whole family.* Discuss what might happen if a fire should start, and be sure everyone knows what to do. Smaller children, especially, should be instructed about what to do in the event of fire.

4. *Inspect your home for escape routes.* Be sure every room, especially bedrooms, has a secondary escape route in the event of a fire blocking the halls or stairwells. Rope ladders can be used in second floor rooms for this purpose.

5. *Instruct your family about what to do in case of fire.* Don't open a closed door during a fire unless you first feel it to see that it isn't hot. If it is not hot, open it slowly to be sure there isn't smoke on the other side. Get to the floor; smoke and heat rise, and in the event of a smoky fire, one can breathe easier near the floor.

Many people panic in a fire situation because they don't know what to do. On the other hand, too much talk about the dangers of fire around small children can frighten them and cause nightmares.

An effective family fire drill is designed to solve both of these problems. First, it instructs everyone on how to act in case of fire and helps eliminate the possibility of panic. Second, if the drill is presented as a game, much of the fear that a child might develop can be eliminated.

Begin by explaining to your family that even though you don't expect fires, they can happen, and that if one should occur, everyone needs to know exactly what to do. Then discuss the ways to get out of the house from each room in the house. Be sure there are two escape routes from each room (usually one through the door and the other through a window).

Windows should open easily. In a child's or an invalid's bedroom, the occupants must be able to open the windows easily without help. A roof outside of a second floor window, a rope ladder, or a nearby tree are effective alternate escape routes.

During the family fire drill, each person should demonstrate that he or she can use the alternate escape route. Instruct everyone to leave the house by this route and then to meet at an appointed spot outside of the house. Stress that it is always important for the whole family to meet at this spot as soon as possible.

Emphasize that in the event of fire everyone is to get out of the house quickly. They are not to worry about saving valuables or how they are dressed. Once out of the house, everyone is to stay there.

Finally, discuss how to contact the fire department. If there is a nearby alarm box, be sure everyone knows where it is and how to operate it. If the fire department must be phoned, discuss the phone number of the fire department, what information to include in your call, and how to give the location of your house.

These discussions and occasional fire drills may one day save the life of a member of your family.

FIRE EXTINGUISHERS

Fire extinguishers keep small fires from becoming roaring blazes. Fire extinguishers that are stored at key points around your home make good sense, but all fire extinguishers are not alike. And using the wrong fire extinguisher on a fire could prove worse than using no extinguisher at all.

When shopping for a fire extinguisher, be sure the unit has either the Underwriters' Laboratories or Factory Mutual seal, which guarantees that the unit meets certain minimum standards.

Your next concern is the classification code of the fire extinguisher, which is usually located next to the approval seal on the label. The code consists of letters which refer to the type of fire the unit can be used on and numbers which indicate the size fire it can fight.

Underwriters' Laboratories has four designations for fires:

    A—Ordinary combustibles such as wood, paper, and cloth
    B—Grease, gasoline, oil, flammable chemicals
    C—Fires involving electrical current
    D—Fires involving combustible metals

Water can be used to put out a Class A fire, but water may cause a Class B (grease) fire to explode. Water on a fire involving a live electrical line might be fatal to the fire fighter.

A typical classification on a fire extinguisher might be 5-B;C. The "5" indicates the size of the fire. The "B" means the extinguisher can be used on grease fires; the "C" means it can be used on electrical fires. A unit rated 1-B will handle a fire involving 3 gallons of flammable fluid; one rated 2-B will handle a fire twice as large. A "5" is a fairly large unit for a home, while a "10" is one of the largest portable units available.

The National Fire Protection Association recommends that you have a 1-A and a 5-B;C unit for each 3,000 square feet of floor area. However, the big point is to have an extinguisher handy when and where you need it—and that may have nothing to do with square feet.

You should have an extinguisher in the bedroom area and another near the living room, since half of all home fires start in these two places.

Grease and flammable liquid fires most often start in the kitchen, garage, basement, or workshop. An extinguisher in each of these areas will provide maximum protection. If you are installing only one unit, put it in or very near the kitchen.

Electric fires can start anywhere in the house. This means that you should have at least one extinguisher that carries a "C" rating.

Most hardware and home center stores carry fire extinguishers, and the major mail order companies carry fairly complete lines. The types most commonly available are pressurized containers with dry powder or carbon dioxide charges. You will find them with ABC and BC ratings, and in sizes from 2 to 10, as a rule. Larger units are available on special order.

You can also buy large extinguishers which hold 2½ gallons of water and are hand pumped for pressure or similar extinguishers that are inverted for operation. When inverted, chemicals in the extinguisher mix to create carbon dioxide which provides water pressure. These latter units are commonly used in schools and industrial areas and are generally considered cumbersome for home use.

For all-around convenience and versatility, the best buy for home use would be an ABC unit with a dry powder charge. A unit rated 2A;10B;C might have a range of 25 feet, discharge in about 10 seconds, and weigh about 10 pounds. The container would be about 20 inches high and would come with a wall bracket. Such units might cost $25 to $30.

For about half that price, you can buy a 5B;C rated unit which would be quite adequate for all kitchen, basement, and garage uses.

Most of these units are designed for one-time use, but they can be recharged by a professional with the proper equipment. Each has a safety pin or protective tape seal, which must be removed before use, and each can be tested by pushing a small pin at the top of the extinguisher. If the pin fails to returns to its original position after been depressed, the extinguisher should be replaced. The more expensive units may have pressure gauges to indicate whether the unit has sufficient pressure.

Buying fire extinguishers and mounting them in easily accessible places are excellent steps towards better home security, but don't stop there. Read the instructions accompanying the extinguishers, not only to yourself but to anyone in the house who might eventually use the unit.

Check out any safety pins or tapes that should be removed before use; check the mode of operation. With some units, you must squeeze the handle; with others you depress a lever. Whatever the method, the operation is quick and simple if you know about it before an emergency.

Finally, when buying fire extinguishers, avoid the small squeeze-bottle and beer can types. They are so small that their effectiveness is limited, and their presence may lull you into a false sense of security.

More than 1,500 homes burn each day in the United States; the total annual bill for damage due to fire runs into the billions.

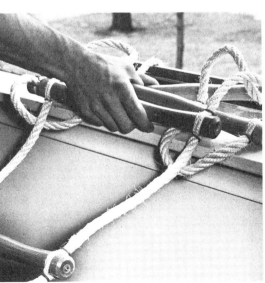

Second floor bedrooms which do not open onto a roof should have some means of escape for the occupants, should fire block escape through the door. Rope ladders designed for this purpose are inexpensive and can be stored on a closet floor. A 1¼-inch thick pole through the end rings is sufficient to anchor the ladder against the window frame.

Left:
Electrically caused fires
start from situations such as
this. When too many plugs
draw current from one wall
outlet, the wires within the
walls overheat. Don't put
more than two plugs in any
wall socket.

Right:
Many community service
organizations and fire
departments are distributing
red ball decals. The number
of decals on a bedroom
window tells firemen how
many children sleep in that
room. The same decal on a
front door indicates that an
elderly person or invalid
lives in the house.

Left:
Always have a screen in
front of your fireplace, and
never have a fire lighted
unless the screen is closed.
Popping sparks have been
the cause of too many fires,
to say nothing of scorched
carpeting.

Right:
The hood over the kitchen
stove should be cleaned
regularly. Grease fires in the
kitchen are one of the
leading types of home fires.

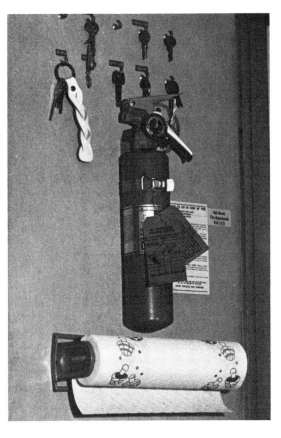

Left:
A fire extinguisher should be stored in or near the kitchen. It should be the dry type used to fight grease fires.

Right:
Closet light bulbs have bad reputations for starting fires. Closet shelves often have much more than this stored on them, and each item brings the stack closer to the hot light bulb. One day someone may forget to turn out the light, and a little while later, a fire may start. Use a low-wattage bulb in closets, keep shelves fairly clear, and make sure the bulbs are nowhere near the stored items.

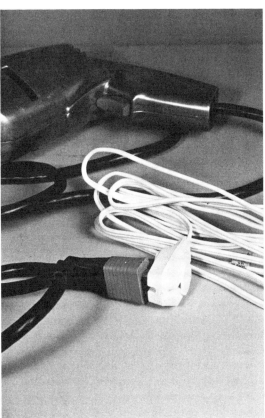

Left:
The manufacturer of this electric drill put a good, heavy-duty cord on it because it needs this kind of cord for safe operation. Do not run it using a light-weight extension cord; always use heavy-duty extension cords with heavy-duty tools.

Right:
Never pull a plug from a wall outlet by grabbing the cord. You may pull the wire out, leaving the plug in the wall. Always grasp the plug itself with your fingers.

Safety Means Security

The pictures and captions on this and the next few pages are a kind of quiz. The object is to see how many of these situations, good and bad, you can identify as existing in your home. A perfect score is next to impossible, but you can try.

Left:
Kitchen falls rate high as a type of home accident. Slippery kitchen floors can be made safe by covering the main traffic areas with a non-skid plastic runner. This is an especially good idea if there are elderly people in the house.

Right:
Dark stairways are dangerous. This one is well lighted, each step is evenly illuminated, and there are no tricky shadows to fool you.

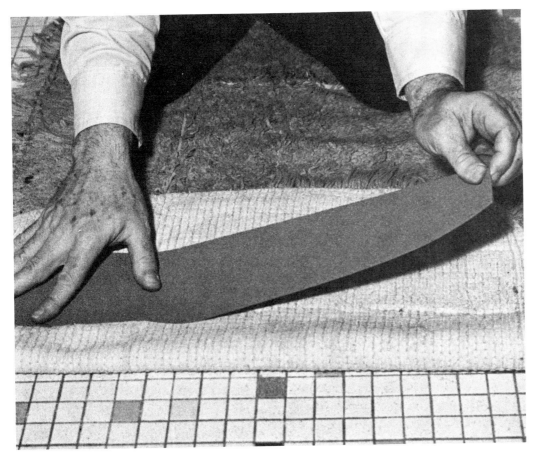

Area rugs, particularly bathroom throw rugs, are always getting tangled up in someone's feet. Apply a wide band of non-skid tape to each end of the rugs to make them more manageable.

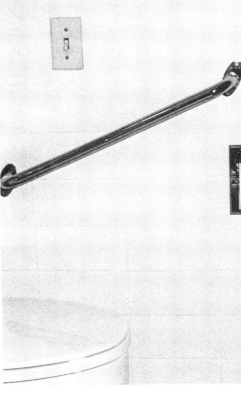

One age-old problem with bathtubs is that if you start to fall, there is nothing to grab. Grab bars make it safe to stand, get up, and climb out of a tub. A grab bar installed next to the toilet is especially useful.

Left:
Attach a non-skid material to the bottom of the tub to prevent falls. These flowers are pretty, but other designs are available, including plain white strips.

Right:
More than 22,000 persons were treated for cleaning agent injuries in one year, and two-thirds of these were children. Put a lock on the cabinet in which you keep cleaning agents. If the statistics are correct, then this cabinet needs a lock more than the medicine cabinet does.

Don't keep bottles around with anything in them unless there is a label telling you what is in the bottle. If you run across an unlabeled bottle, throw it out. Don't take chances guessing its contents.

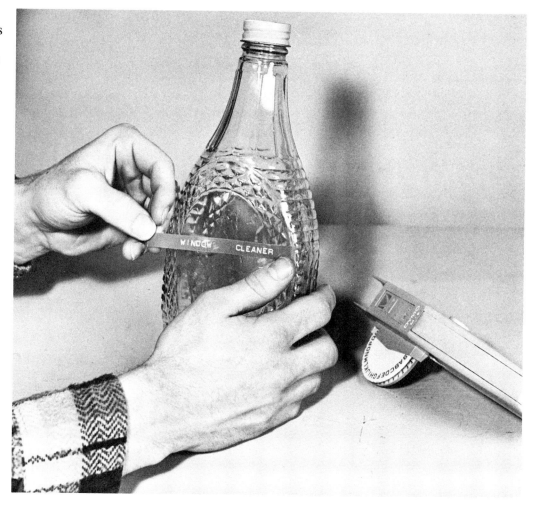

Cleaning your locks in a solvent such as turpentine will permit them to work better. But use solvents only in a well-ventilated place. Basements are usually not well ventilated.

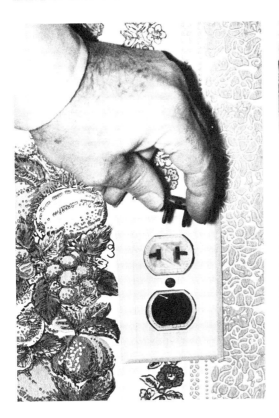

Left:
Children love to stick objects and fingers into wall outlets. Guard your children against possible shock by inserting plastic caps into the socket.

Right:
Reglaze all storm doors with plastic panes. Many state laws now require this practice.

Wear heavy gloves when handling broken glass.

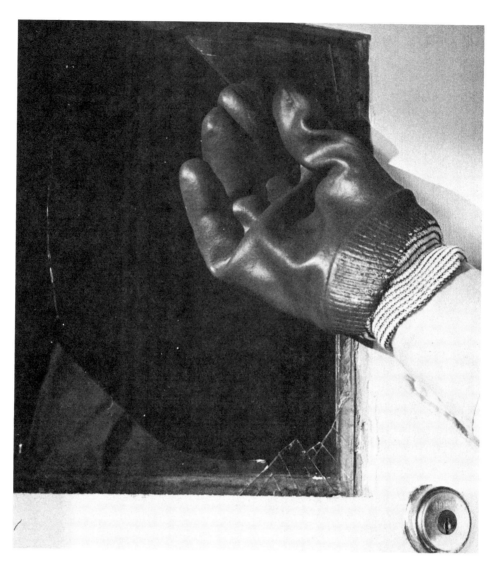

Left:
Small pieces of broken glass are worse than big pieces. When removing a broken light bulb, use a thermos bottle cork, a wadded up cloth, or some other protective item to force the bulb base to turn. Don't turn it with your bare fingers.

Right:
There is almost nothing that would help a burglar more than to find an extension ladder lying beside your garage, a common storage spot for ladders. If you do store your ladder outside, lock it up.

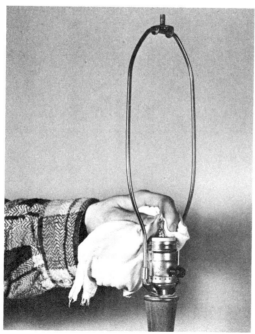

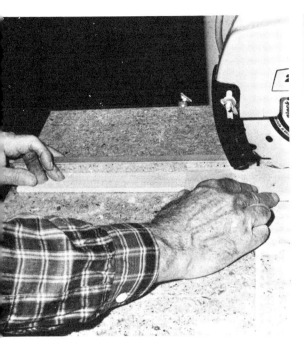 

Left:
Keep fingers away from power saw blades. Use a "pusher" to feed the piece of wood being cut toward the radial saw.

Right:
When you see a crack in a concrete step, make plans to fix it quickly. The crack will grow worse and someday someone will step on it and the whole piece may give way.

Long steps offer special problems. They must have handrails, preferably on both sides. Exterior steps should be sanded to prevent someone slipping in the event of snow or ice. All exterior steps should be lighted at night, and they must be maintained regularly. A fall here would be especially dangerous.

This passageway between two walls is narrow and dark. One way to make it safe from intruders is to put a locked gate on it.

Left:
Every stairway, particularly basement steps, should have a handrail. All handrails should be firmly attached to the wall.

Right:
This patio needs a step, but the solution used here is worse than the original problem. The concrete block doesn't provide firm footing and could cause a severe fall.

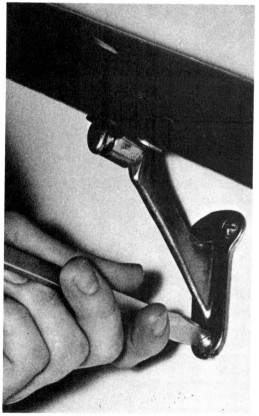

All outbuildings should be kept locked, not only for security reasons, but also to prevent small children from wandering in and hurting themselves on the stored equipment.

Those cellar doors need to be well made and securely locked from the inside. The safest cellar doors of this type are made of steel.

When working with sanders, saws, and other tools which produce chips or sawdust, always wear safety goggles. They are inexpensive and may save you from a painful injury. Eye injuries account for one of the chief kinds of injuries listed each year.

The easy and safe way to put up a long ladder is to walk as shown here; don't attempt to lift and carry it.

Left:
Keep the base of the ladder far enough from the house to allow a safe angle for climbing.

Right:
Always check the footing of the ladder once it is in position. If both feet aren't in solid contact with the ground, reposition the ladder.

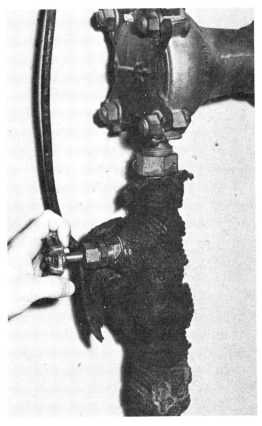

In an emergency at your house, you may have to turn off the water, the electricity, or the gas. Do you know where and how to operate the controls for each of these necessities in your home?

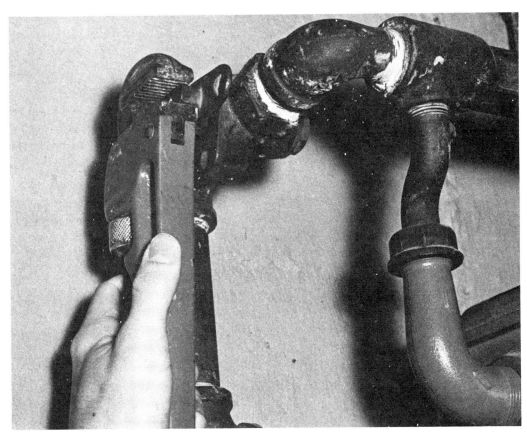

When You Travel

Empty houses have a special appearance; it is hard to hide the fact that no one is at home. That is the whole problem when you head out on your vacation—how do you make your house look alive and lived in? Here are a few ways:

1. Ask a neighbor to park his car in your driveway from time to time. Perhaps he can leave his car there overnight.

2. In the winter after a snowfall, have someone drive in and out of the driveway a few times to make tire tracks.

3. Don't let newspapers or mail accumulate; have a neighbor pick them up. If you arrange to stop mail or delivery service, you are notifying a group of people that you are going away.

4. Don't tell the local newspaper about the great trip to Hawaii you are going to make. Wait until you come back, and then tell the world where you've been.

5. Invest in three or four automatic timers, and set them so that lights go on and off in the living room, then on and off in the bathroom, and then on and off in the bedroom. When one light goes off, plan for the light in the next room to switch on a few seconds later. Lights burning all night are an obvious sign that you aren't there, and lights seldom remain on in the same room when you're at home.

6. Attach one timer to a radio and let it turn on and off. One of the things that makes a house feel empty is the silence.

7. Set the automatic garage door switch so that it can't be opened by remote control, but only by the switch inside the garage. This will prevent accidental opening of the door.

8. Have someone cut your grass while you're gone.

9. Suspend your telephone service. The operator will tell all callers that service has been temporarily disconnected. Some of your friends may think you haven't paid your telephone bill. Perhaps a burglar will think that, too.

10. If you have a telephone answering device, you might leave your phone service on and program the tape to say that you are unavailable but will return the call shortly. This will discourage the burglar who operates by phoning until he finds a place where no one answers and then hurries over to rob that house.

Before you leave for any length of time, improve security by putting police bars on all but one exterior door and by putting away anything of value that might be seen from a window.

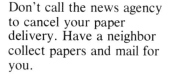

Don't call the news agency to cancel your paper delivery. Have a neighbor collect papers and mail for you.

Use several timers on several lamps in different parts of the house. Program them to go on and off in a natural sequence. A light that remains on all night long won't fool a burglar. Be sure the timers cannot be seen from a window.

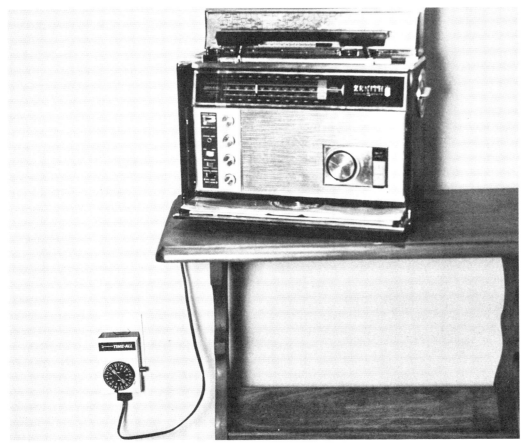

Use a timer to turn on a radio or television set. Some of the noise may be heard outside of the house and may suggest that someone is at home.

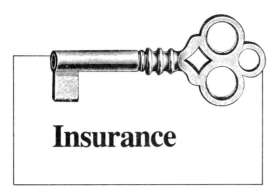

Insurance

Fires and burglaries in the United States result in a staggering annual loss of more than $1.5 billion dollars. If it weren't for the protection provided by insurance, the majority of this loss would have to come from the pockets of average homeowners. That's why your insurance program is an important part of the security of your home; it provides financial security when you fall victim to a particular hazard.

It is vital to know that you have the right insurance coverage, whether you own your home, rent a house or apartment, or own a condominium. To know this, you should understand what your insurance policies cover and what they do not cover. Property values are constantly changing; you should review your insurance every year or so to make sure you have not become underinsured.

HOMEOWNER'S INSURANCE

Homeowner's insurance protects you in the event of fire, theft, windstorm, and other hazards. Few people take the time to understand this type of coverage, but you should do so because it can make a great financial difference in the event of a severe loss. Remember these basic facts about homeowner's insurance:

• Six different varieties of homeowner policies are available. They are generally referred to as HO-1, HO-2, and so on through HO-6. Not every company sells all six.

• HO-1 is the basic fire and theft policy for homeowners. HO-2, HO-3, and HO-5 are progressively better policies for homeowners, with each one offering better coverage, at higher cost, than the previous policy. HO-5 is called the All-Risk policy because it covers all risks except those specifically excluded in the wording of the policy.

• HO-4 is a policy written specifically for people who rent homes or apartments.

• HO-6 is a policy written specifically for people who own condominiums.

• A "risk" in insurance terminology is a type of hazard. Fire is a risk, and windstorm is another. Insurance companies have identified 18 separate risks or perils they will insure against. Note that each peril is separately named or excluded in each policy. Actually, a homeowner policy is a collection of individual policies covering certain, but not necessarily all, of these perils.

Most insurance companies will insure your home against the following perils:

1. Fire, lightning
2. Damage to property removed from premises endangered by fire
3. Windstorm, hail
4. Explosion
5. Riot
6. Damage by aircraft
7. Damage by vehicles not owned or operated by persons covered by the policy
8. Damage from smoke
9. Vandalism, malicious mischief
10. Glass breakage
11. Theft
12. Falling objects
13. Weight of snow, ice
14. Collapse of the building or part of it
15. Bursting or cracking of steam or hot water heating system or of appliances for heating water
16. Leakage or overflow of water from plumbing, heating, or air conditioning
17. Freezing of plumbing, heating, air conditioning systems, and domestic appliances
18. Damage from short circuits and other accidentally generated currents to electrical appliances, devices, fixtures and wiring (excluding tubes, transistors, and similar electronic components)

• Every policy has certain special limits of liability. These limits are the maximum amount a policy will pay for

Perils Generally Covered by Homeowner Policies

HO-1 Perils 1 through 11

HO-2 Perils 1 through 18

HO-3 Perils 1 through 18 on personal property, except 10 (glass breakage). All risks on buildings except those specifically excluded in the policy.

HO-4 For those who rent. Perils 1 through 18 on personal property, except 10 (glass breakage).

HO-5 All risks except those which are specifically excluded in the policy.

HO-6 For owners of condominiums. Perils 1 through 18, except 10 (glass breakage).

Not all companies identify their policies with these numbers, but all follow the same plan. Your insurance agent can identify the type of policy. Most policies are reasonably standard, though some differ in slight respects. Policy conditions also may vary because of state regulations.

certain losses. These include 1) a maximum of $100 on money, bullion, stamp collections, bank notes; 2) a maximum of $500 on securities, bills, deeds, tickets, etc.; 3) a maximum of $1,000 on manuscripts; 4) a maximum of $500 for theft of jewelry and furs; 5) a maximum of $500 for boats, boat trailers, and boating equipment; and 6) a maximum of $500 for a trailer. If you have things in these categories which have a greater value than these limits, you must insure them separately.

• If you have an office in your home or do any kind of business from your home, the business equipment is probably not covered by your homeowner policy. It must be covered in a separate policy.

• Homeowner insurance premiums vary from locality to locality and are determined by the protection you ask for, the amount of insurance, the construction of your home, and the company with which you are insuring. The rate is also affected by whether you live in a high-or low-crime area and what type of fire protection your community offers. Each community is rated and this rate affects your premiums.

• Homeowner's insurance can be difficult or even impossible to get. If you have had too many losses, for example, your policy may be cancelled or not renewed. If your house is considered a high risk, you may have difficulty finding an insurer.

FLOOD INSURANCE

No homeowner policy covers flood damage, but some protection may be available through insurance programs sponsored or partially supported by the federal government.

Flood insurance is available only in communities which have undertaken certain flood control measures required by the government. In these communities, the flood insurance is sold by private insurance companies at government-subsidized premium rates. You may be able to buy up to $35,000 of flood insurance on a house and up to $10,000 on personal property.

HIGH-CRIME AREAS

In many instances, private insurance companies have backed away from offering insurance in areas where a high crime rate has caused exceptionally high losses. The federal government makes up to $10,000 of burglary and robbery insurance available to homeowners and tenants in certain states. The premiums for such coverage ranges from $60 to $80 per year, depending on the crime rate of the area. States involved in this federal program include Connecticut, Delaware, Florida, Illinois, Kansas, Maryland, Massachusetts, Missouri, New Jersey, New York, Ohio, Pennsylvania, Rhode Island, Tennessee, and the District of Columbia.

To qualify for this insurance, you must equip your home or apartment with certain types of locks. For information, write to Safety Management Institute,

Federal Crime Insurance, P.O. Box 41033, Washington, D.C. 20014.

COVERAGE AND INFLATION

Insurance companies say that if you haven't reviewed your policy and increased your coverage within the last couple of years, you probably don't have enough insurance. The cost of replacing your home, if it were totally destroyed, has risen sharply while the amount of your insurance policy has remained the same.

Building costs vary sharply from area to area, but no matter where you live, they have almost surely gone up. If your house cost $25,000 to build in 1960, it could cost as much as $50,000 to $55,000 to replace today. If you haven't changed your homeowner policy during this period and you suffer a serious fire, your insurance proceeds are likely to be far, far short of your needs.

To solve this problem, first review your homeowner policy. Determine what it would cost to replace your home, either by discussing the problem with your insurance agent or by having the house appraised. You can't get an accurate, to-the-penny figure, of course, but you can come close to what you would need to rebuild your house.

Many insurance companies have become concerned over the inflation problem and have begun to offer special policy arrangements in which the coverage of the policy is increased each year, either by a fixed percentage or in step with construction-cost index figures published by the U.S. Department of Commerce. Ask your insurance agent about such plans.

THE 80 PERCENT RULE

If you insure your house for at least 80 percent of its replacement cost, the company will pay the full cost of restoring the house to its original condition if it is damaged by one of the listed perils.

If you insure for less than 80 percent of the replacement cost, the company will settle in one of two ways. It may give you "actual cash value," which means it will pay the replacement cost minus an allowance for depreciation. Or the company may pay a proportion of the replacement cost computed on the ratio of your insurance to the 80 percent figure.

In other words, if 80 percent of the replacement cost of your home is $30,000, and you insure for only $20,000, you would receive two-thirds of $20,000, or about $13,500.

On the other hand, if you insure for 80 percent of the replacement cost, the computation is different.

Suppose your house cost $35,000 to build 10 years ago. At the time, you bought a policy covering 80 percent of its value. The face value of this policy thus was $28,000.

If you had suffered a total-loss fire that first year, the insurance company would have paid whatever amount was necessary to restore the structure to its original condition—up to the $28,000 face amount. There would be no deduction for depreciation, and the $28,000 would have been ample to do the job at that time.

But now suppose you have a total-loss fire this year—10 years later—and you haven't changed your policy during this time. Because of inflation, it will now take $55,000 to replace your house—but your policy still has a face value of $28,000.

In the settlement, the insurance company still will not deduct for depreciation—because you originally insured under the 80 percent rule—but it will not pay more than the face amount of $28,000. You'll have to bear the difference ($37,000) yourself.

However, if you had reviewed your policy last year, and upgraded the face amount to 80 percent *of the current replacement cost*, the company would pay the entire rebuilding cost—up to the face amount.

This little illustration clearly shows why you should review your homeowner's policy every year or so. Your insurance agent will help you to determine what your replacements costs might be, and what the new face amount of the policy should be.

Keep in mind that the company is never liable for more than the face value of the policy. If it costs you $30,000 to rebuild your home after a fire, and you have insured for $28,000 (which is more than the required 80 percent), you will still not receive more than $28,000 under any circumstances.

When you compute what it would cost you to replace your home, don't include the cost of the land, the foundation, underground pipes, or other items not likely to be damaged by the perils covered by the policy. But keep in mind that a part of the repair cost will be tearing out damaged materials and hauling them away.

PERSONAL PROPERTY LOSSES

Replacement costs apply only to your house structure and not to personal property such as furniture and clothing. If a fire invades your home, it is likely you will have both building and personal property damage. There will be two settlements, one to cover the building and the other to cover the personal property.

For your personal property losses, the insurance company will give you "actual cash value," which means that it will take each item's replacement cost and deduct a depreciation amount.

Homeowner policies cover the furnishings and clothing around the average house. A typical living room chair or dining room table, for example, would be included. An extremely valuable antique chair or table, however, would be covered only at nominal value and not at its antique value unless you insured it separately.

Everything in your house is covered by your homeowner insurance policy, even if it belongs to someone else, such as a guest or someone working for you. But it is wise to take a little time to read your policy, for you will find some exclusions which may surprise you. Your automobile is not included, nor is a go-cart you might have in your garage. On the other hand, a garden tractor or lawn mower is covered.

PREMIUM DISCOUNTS

Some insurance companies, concerned about the rising theft losses, are encouraging policy holders to install alarm systems by offering premium discounts to homeowners who have alarm systems. The terms of the discount vary from company to company, but there are usually two types of discount offered. One is for a home with an alarm system that is self-contained. The second discount is for a home that has an alarm system connected either to a police or fire station switchboard or to the switchboard of a private security agency.

Premium discounts generally apply to burglar alarm systems, although some insurance companies will offer discounts for homeowners who install fire alarm systems. Explore the benefits your insurance company has to offer.

INSURANCE CLAIMS

Most claims against homeowner policies are settled fairly within a reasonable length of time and with a minimum of trouble. But problems can and do arise. Misunderstandings often occur because the insured doesn't know the terms of his policy or what he is entitled to collect. Too often, a homeowner thinks he is completely insured and that he will receive full replacement for every bit of his loss.

His first shock comes when he discovers that personal effects (furniture and clothing) are paid for at "actual cash value," which is actual value less an amount for depreciation. The amount the insurance company offers him often turns out to be much less than he expected, and he feels cheated.

The next shock may come when the homeowner discovers that the cost of rebuilding his house has risen sharply, and that his policy will pay him only a part of this cost. He may not have insured for 80 percent, or if he did, he may not have increased the face value of the policy for a number of years.

The homeowner may also be disillusioned because the claims adjuster sticks strictly to the terms of the policy and makes every effort to keep the amount the company pays out as low as possible.

Finally, the time required to settle the claim may seem outrageously lengthy to the homeowner, even though it actually isn't long in insurance settlement terms. A major loss from a peril, such as fire, produces a complex situation, reams of paperwork, and a good deal of discussion, confirmation, and debate. To make matters worse, all of this occurs at a time when the homeowner's house is in ruins, his life disrupted, and the whole world seems upside down.

Much of the pain can be avoided if you are prepared for a claim before the need arises. Here are some things to do that will help:

1. *Know your insurance policies.* Read them or sit down with your insurance agent and discuss them. Know what is and what is not covered in each policy. Find out how his company settles claims.

2. *Make sure that the face value of your insurance is updated* in keeping with current inflated costs.

3. *Discuss depreciation with your insurance agent*, so that you understand how it applies and what it might mean in case of a claim. Remember that if you lose a 5-year-old couch, you will receive the cost of the couch less an amount for depreciation, but you will still have to replace the couch at current prices.

4. *Make a list of your valuable possessions.* There is no way that you will ever be able to sit down and list every item in your home after a fire. It would be helpful if you made a list of the major items— furniture, television sets, appliances, etc.—showing when they were purchased and how much they cost. It helps

to record serial and model numbers, too. Your claims adjuster can work to settle this part of the claim much faster with this information to work with.

5. *File a photograph of major items*, especially if they are of considerable value. This is good verification for use in claim settlements.

6. *Report your claim immediately* and produce your documentation promptly. This will move the paperwork along.

7. *Don't exaggerate the claim amount.* Don't turn a $300 television set into a $595 model. Some people do this because they feel they lose too much through the depreciation computation. Such inflated claims usually are discovered, and the existence of one will cause the adjuster to double-check the price claims on every item. The result can be a much slower settlement.

Changes in Insurance Policies

The information in this chapter is a general discussion of insurance for homeowners; some details may differ in your locality for a number of reasons. In addition, changes in policies and coverages are made from time to time. Use the material in this chapter as a general guide, but check specific details with a local insurance agent who can give you exact terms currently in effect.

Standard Amounts of Insurance for Homeowner Policies

Type of policy	House, attached structures	Detached structures	Trees, shrubs, plants	Personal property on premises	Additional living expenses
HO-1	Minimum $8,000, based on property value	10% of amount of insurance on house	$250 max. per item, up to 5% of insurance on house	50% of insurance on house	10% of insurance on house
HO-2	Same	Same	Same	Same	20% of insurance on house
HO-3	Same	Same	Same	Same	20% of insurance on house
HO-4	10% of personal property insurance on additions and alterations to unit	None	$250 max. per item, up to 10% of personal property insurance	Minimum $4,000, based on value of property	20% of personal property insurance
HO-5	Minimum $15,000, based on property value	10% of amount of insurance on house	$250 max. per item up to 5% of amount of insurance on house	50% of insurance on house	20% of insurance on house
HO-6	$1,000 on owner's additions and alterations	None	$250 max. per item, up to 10% of personal property insurance	$4,000 minimum, based on value of property	40% of personal property insurance

Comprehensive Personal Liability: $25,000 on all HO Forms.

Medical Payments: $500 per person, up to $25,000 for all injured in same accident—on all HO Forms.

Damage to Property of Others: $250 on all HO Forms.

Special Limits of Liability: Same on all HO Forms (See description in text).

Personal Property away from Premises: 10% of personal property insurance (minimum $1,000) on all HO Forms except HO-5, in which coverage is 50% of amount of insurance on the house.

Index